D1415873

THE SAFE DOG
HANDBOOK

Melanie Monteiro

THE SAFE DOG
HANDBOOK

A COMPLETE GUIDE
to Protecting Your Pooch,
Indoors and Out

CRESTLINE

This edition published in 2011 by CRESTLINE
A division of BOOK SALES, INC.
276 Fifth Avenue Suite 206
New York, New York 10001
USA

This edition published by arrangement with Quarry Books, a member of the Quayside Publishing Group.

© 2009 Melanie Monteiro

All rights reserved. No part of this book may be reproduced in any form without written permission of the copyright owners. All images in this book have been reproduced with the knowledge and prior consent of the artists concerned, and no responsibility is accepted by the producer, publisher, or printer for any infringement of copyright or otherwise, arising from the contents of this publication. Every effort has been made to ensure that credits accurately comply with information supplied. We apologize for any inaccuracies that may have occurred and will resolve inaccurate or missing information in a subsequent reprinting of the book.

First published in the United States of America by
Quarry Books, a member of
Quayside Publishing Group
100 Cummings Center, Suite 406-L
Beverly, Massachusetts 01915-6101
Telephone: (978) 282-9590
Fax: (978) 283-2742
www.quarrybooks.com

Library of Congress Cataloging-in-Publication Data
Monteiro, Melanie.
  The safe dog handbook : a complete guide to protecting your pooch,
indoors and out / Melanie Monteiro.
     p. cm.
  1. Dogs--Safety measures. 2. Dogs--Wounds and injuries--Treatment.
  3. First aid for animals. I. Title.

  SF427.M723 2009
  636.7'0893--dc22

                                        2008033114
                                           CIP

ISBN-13: 978-0-7858-2810-5

The Safe Dog Handbook contains a variety of tips and recommendations for your dog. While caution was taken to give safe recommendations, it is impossible to predict the outcome of each suggestion. Neither Melanie Monteiro, nor the publisher, Quayside Publishing Group, accepts liability for any mental, financial, or physical harm that arises from following the advice or techniques, or use of the procedures in this book. Readers should use personal judgment when applying the recommendations of this text.

10 9 8 7 6 5 4 3 2 1

Design: Rachel Fitzgibbon, studio rkf
Cover image: Erin Vey/www.erinvey.com
Back jacket: Nick Ridley/www.nickridley.com, top; Lee Moreno-Lesser, second;
www.istockphoto.com, third & bottom
Illustrations: Colleen Hanlon

Printed in China

For Taiga, dog of a lifetime

contents

introduction

We know their favorite spots to scratch. We know what treats they like best. We even know which funny noises will make them cock their heads. We know so much about the dogs we love. But do we know how to keep them safe?

I used to think I knew all I needed to know about dog safety. Just lock up the rat poison, put away the chocolate, slap on a collar and ID tag, and call it a day. That was about it … until a yellow Lab puppy named Taiga came along and changed everything.

Taiga looked sweet, but there was no mistaking her wild and curious spirit. Just picking her up required the expertise of a greased-pig wrangler.

Outside her crate, I had to watch Taiga's every move—and even then she managed to eat a plastic razor, chip her tooth on a rock, and nip at a bee, leaving her with a head as big as a watermelon, and me in a total panic.

Then one day at five months old, she slipped out the door into the backyard. Minutes later, she was prancing around gleefully with an azalea branch in her mouth, whipping it around like a baton twirler. Watching this adorable display, I suddenly had a faint recollection of hearing … *somewhere* … that azaleas were bad for dogs.

Snatching the branch away, I called the ASPCA Animal Poison Control Center hotline. I was told that eating azalea leaves could kill—yes, *kill*—my puppy! A wave of nausea washed over me as I tried to answer their rapid-fire questions: *How much has she eaten? What are her symptoms? How far away is the nearest vet? Do you have any activated charcoal in the house?*

Eighteen hours and a small fortune in vet bills later, it was determined that thankfully, she had not swallowed any part of the azalea. She was going to be just fine. I, however, was *not* fine. How is it that a person can waltz into any nursery or garden center and, without any warning labels, buy something so toxic?

I was furious, embarrassed, and mortified. What other home hazards was I unaware of? I hit the books, gathering information and interviewing emergency-room vets. I learned that thousands of dogs are hurt or killed in their own homes each year by seemingly innocent everyday items from grapes to golf balls—dogs like Josephine, the sweet Lab puppy who died after chewing a sago palm in her backyard, and Dagney, the tiny mixed-breed who suffered kidney failure after eating a box of raisins.

It's not that this information isn't available—it's just not always easy to find. There might be a dog-proofing chapter in a general book on dog care, or the occasional magazine article. Sometimes veterinary clinics post holiday-time warnings. If you look, you can find information on the Internet. But nearly always, the material is incomplete, poorly organized, or never around when you need it.

So here it is: The first always-around-when-you-need-it, complete safety book for dogs. Here, you'll learn step-by-step how to create a hazard-safe home and garden. You'll learn how to take precautions when you're out and about in the world, how to prepare for an emergency, and what to do if things go wrong. You'll even learn a few tips on how to keep your home and garden looking their best in the midst of furniture chewers, door scratchers, carpet tinklers, and dirt diggers.

But before you dive in, I want to reassure you that for every dog that suffers an unfortunate accident, there are countless more who live long, happy lives without ever seeing the inside of an emergency room. I hope this book helps your dog to be one of them.

—Melanie Monteiro

one

PREVENTION AND SAFETY OVERVIEW

From the candy dish on the coffee table to the foxgloves in the flowerpot, the average home contains numerous safety hazards for dogs and puppies. But protecting your pooch isn't as difficult as you might think—it just takes a little effort up front. Luckily for your dog, you're up to the task, or you wouldn't be holding this book! This chapter will teach you how to lay the groundwork for overall safety: learning the basics of prevention and prepared-ness, and setting yourself up for a successful outcome if you are ever faced with an emergency.

Preparing Your Emergency Information

Imagine you've just come home to find your trash knocked over, vomit on the kitchen floor, and your dog listless and unable to stand. Who will you call for help? Depending on the time, day, and type of emergency, the answer might not always be the same. Many regular veterinary clinics don't keep emergency hours, and designated emergency clinics are often open only on nights and weekends. Assembling the right information now—*before* an emergency—is a critical step in getting your dog fast treatment.

STEP 1: WRITE THE FOLLOWING INFORMATION ON INDEX CARDS:

Your Regular Veterinarian
Name
Phone number
Address/Directions
Hours of Operation
Drive time in moderate traffic

Emergency Clinic
Name
Phone number
Address/Directions
Hours of Operation
Drive time in moderate traffic

Microchip or Tattoo Information
Registering company
Phone number
Your dog's ID number

24-Hour Animal Poison Control Center Hotline
For poison-related emergencies, call the ASPCA Animal Poison Control Center hotline. Veterinary toxicologists are available 24 hours a day, 365 days a year, and can quickly assess the seriousness of the situation based on your dog's weight, age, and type and amount of poison ingested. They'll guide you through the steps to take immediately, such as how to induce vomiting, and even call your vet's office or emergency clinic to advise the staff prior to your arrival. After they've helped you, they will ask for a credit card number for a reasonable consultation fee.

In North America: ASPCA's 24-hour Animal Poison Control Center 888.426.4435 *(Long distance charges may apply if calling outside of North America)*

In the United Kingdom: Vetfone 24-Hour Helpline: 09065 00 55 00
This helpline is staffed 24/7 by qualified veterinary nurses with access to a pet poison database. A nominal per-minute charge applies. Inquire about the fee when you call.

Outside North America/United Kingdom: Ask your veterinarian for the best number to call in a poison emergency.

STEP 2: POST THE ABOVE INFORMATION.
Post an index card near your main home telephone. Keep an additional copy in your wallet or purse. Enter all information into your cell phone and/or PDA. (Consider transcribing the information on the inside cover of this book.)

STEP 3: BOOKMARK THE EMERGENCY FIRST AID SECTION OF THIS BOOK.
Place a bookmark or otherwise mark the beginning of the Emergency First Aid chapter (page 118) for quick reference.

STEP 4: KEEP THIS BOOK WITH YOUR DOG'S SUPPLIES—NOT HIDDEN ON THE BOOKSHELF!
If this book is tucked away on a bookshelf, it might not be easily accessed in an emergency. Pick a spot, such as with the dog's first-aid kit (see page 12), and keep it there.

Learning the Basics of First Aid

In the first moments following an emergency, your dog's life may depend on your ability to respond swiftly and properly until you can get him professional veterinary treatment. Prepare in advance by taking a hands-on pet first-aid course and periodically studying the first-aid chapter of this book (see page 118), where you'll learn critical skills including canine CPR, the Heimlich maneuver, treating shock, inducing vomiting, restraining an injured dog, and safe transportation techniques (see Resources, page 157, for information on pet first-aid courses).

ASSEMBLING A DOG'S FIRST AID KIT

Most of the items needed for a first-aid kit for dogs can be found at a drugstore or in one of the many ready-made kits available from pet supply stores. In either case, the kit should be supplemented with a few specialty items that can be ordered online. Store the complete kit in a clearly labeled lidded storage container, toolbox, or small duffle bag and keep in a cool, dry, accessible place. (The Emergency First Aid section [pages 118-147] includes instructions for how and when to use the following items.)

Commercial Muzzle or Panty Hose, Gauze, or Fabric Strip About 24 to 36-inches (0.6 to 0.9 m) Long
To prevent a scared, injured dog from biting during critical treatment

Hydrogen Peroxide (3 percent)
Given orally to induce vomiting in noncaustic poisoning emergencies at a dose of 1 to 2 teaspoons (5 to 10 ml) per 10 pounds (5 kg) of body weight. *Use only with a vet's approval and guidance.*

Toxiban or Other Vet-Approved Activated Charcoal
Helps absorb ingested poisons. *Use only under a vet's guidance*

Turkey Baster or Oral Syringe
Can be used to administer activated charcoal and other oral liquid medications

Tweezers and Needle-Nose Pliers, Forceps, or Hemostat
For removing foreign objects from the mouth and throat

Diphenhydramine Antihistamine (such as Benadryl)
The correct dose is 1 milligram per pound of body weight (e.g., one 25-mg tablet for a 25-pound [11.4 kg] dog.) *Use only with a vet's approval to treat allergic reactions.*

Saline Eye Wash
For flushing irritants/toxins from a dog's eyes

Mild, Grease-Cutting Dish Soap
For washing topical irritants and caustic substances off a dog's coat

Rubber Gloves
To protect yourself while treating topical poisonings or electric shock accidents

Pediatric Rectal Thermometer and Water-Based Lubricant or Petroleum Jelly
For measuring a dog's body temperature

Cut and Wound Care Items
- Hand sanitizer
- Antiseptic (povidone-iodine) solution
- Elastic bandage (such as Ace)
- Roll of stretchable gauze
- Nonstick bandages (such as Tefla)
- Sanitary pad (unscented)
- Adhesive tape
- Blunt scissors
- Duct tape

In addition to all the items listed above, this book (bookmarked on the Emergency First Aid section) or another pet first-aid guide should be an essential part of the kit. These books will help guide you in responding to emergencies until a professional takes over.

HYPOGLYCEMIC DOGS
Some dogs, such as young toy-breed puppies or field dogs that work in cold weather, are potential candidates for hypoglycemia (low blood sugar). If your vet feels your dog fits this category, include a packet of honey, glucose paste, or corn syrup in your first-aid kit. During a blood sugar episode such as weakness, seizure, or loss of consciousness, a few drops can be rubbed into the dog's gums to help stabilize him as you transport him to the vet. Consult your vet for further advice on how to treat blood sugar emergencies.

Familiarize yourself with the contents of a ready-made kit so you know how to use them in an emergency. Supplement with any additional items your dog may need such as a breed-specific muzzle or vet-prescribed medications.

IS PET INSURANCE RIGHT FOR YOU?
Unfortunately, for many dog owners the costs for veterinary treatments can run sky high. Unless you have a budget for emergencies or incredibly deep pockets, pet insurance is a wise investment for many caring dog guardians.

Monthly premiums are relatively low, but can vary widely depending on the plan you choose as well as your dog's age, breed, and where you live. It's easy to shop around and get a fast quote by visiting the various providers' websites. Plans range from "accident only" to premium plans that include everything from vaccines and wellness exams to chemotherapy and complex surgeries. A few things that are not usually covered are congenital, hereditary, or pre-existing conditions.

safety tip
Whenever possible, call ahead before transporting a dog to the emergency clinic so they can be prepared for your arrival. On some occasions, such as a long wait time or lack of an antidote, they may recommend another clinic that's better equipped to handle the situation. Always follow the safe transportation advice in the first-aid section (see page 118) and drive carefully with the hazard lights on, if necessary.

Knowing What's Normal—and What's Not

One of the best ways to recognize signs of illness or injury in a dog is to become familiar with his normal appearance and vital signs while he's healthy. Observe his eyes, gait, energy level, and alertness. Look at the color of his gums—they should be pink (if your dog's breed has naturally black-pigmented gums, gently pull down the lower eyelid to check the membrane color instead). Notice his eating, drinking, and elimination habits. Finally, check your dog's vital signs and write down the results. Repeat this process a few times per year, or as needed if your dog's general health changes (see chart, page 15).

BREATHING

Watch a resting dog's chest rise and fall to count his breaths. Count for 15 seconds, then multiply by 4. This is your breaths-per-minute rate. After vigorous exercise, normal respiratory rates are measured in pants per minute.

HEART RATE AND PULSE

Be sure the dog is in a normal, rested state when determining his baseline heart rate. Have him lie down on his right side. Gently bend his front, left elbow toward the chest, and place the palm of your hand on his body at the point where the elbow meets the chest. Count the individual beats for 15 seconds, then multiply by 4. This is your beats-per-minute rate. A dog's pulse can be felt at the same time as each heartbeat. The easiest place to locate the pulse is the femoral artery. Alternately, try feeling the area just above the large, middle pad on the underside of any paw.

Heart rates and pulses that fall outside the normal limits could be signs of an emergency. Be sure to recheck your results for accuracy if you get an abnormal reading (see chart, page 15).

To check the heart rate, have the dog lie on his right side. Bend his front, left elbow toward the chest and place your hand at the point on his body where the elbow meets the chest.

To check the pulse, lightly press two fingers on the inside of either back leg, at the point where the leg meets the groin area, and count the pulses.

RECORDING YOUR DOG'S VITAL SIGNS

While your dog is healthy and rested, practice checking his breathing rate, body temperature, and heart rate/pulse. Write down the results and keep them in your pet first-aid kit for comparison should your dog ever become ill or injured.

NORMAL RESPIRATORY (BREATHING) RATES

Dogs up to 30 lb. (13.6 kg)	10 to 30 breaths per minute/up to 200 pants per minute
Dogs over 30 lb. (13.6 kg)	10 to 30 breaths per minute/up to 200 pants per minute
Puppies	15 to 40 breaths per minute/up to 200 pants per minute

NORMAL HEART RATES

Dogs up to 30 lb (13.6 kg)	100 to 160 beats per minute
Dogs over 30 lb (13.6 kg)	60 to 100 beats per minute
Puppies up to 1 year old	120 to 160 beats per minute

Normal body temperature is 100.2°F to 102.8°F (37.9°C to 39.3°C)

Seek treatment immediately for temperatures below 99°F (37.2°C) or above 104°F (40°C).

TEMPERATURE

To take a dog's temperature, a pediatric digital rectal thermometer works best. Lubricate the tip of the thermometer with a water-based lubricant (such as K-Y) or petroleum jelly. If possible, have a helper restrain the dog using the head/hug method (see page 121). Lift the dog's tail near the base and gently insert the tip of the thermometer into the rectum. If there is no one to help you, you can straddle the dog, facing his rump, and close your legs against his sides to keep him still while you lift his tail and insert the thermometer. Hold it in place until you hear the beep, then remove and wipe with a tissue before reading the results. Be sure to thoroughly sterilize the thermometer afterward.

CAPILLARY REFILL TIME

A quick, easy way to measure blood circulation is with the capillary refill time method. Use a fingertip to apply moderate pressure to the dog's upper gum area and remove it. Watch the fingerprint turn from white back to pink—it should take no more than 2 seconds.

A capillary refill time of less than 1 second or more than 3 seconds is an emergency requiring immediate treatment.

safety tips

signs and situations requiring emergency treatment

The following conditions require immediate, emergency attention:

- Difficulty, abnormal, or no breathing
- Loss of consciousness or collapse
- Shock: weak, rapid pulse; pale gums; cool limbs; low body temperature; prolonged capillary refill time
- Bloat: drooling, swollen abdomen, extreme anxiety or restlessness, pacing, attempting to vomit or defecate unsuccessfully
- Extremes of body temperature
- Extremes of heart rate or pulse
- Blue, pale, yellow, brown, or bright red gums
- Depression, disorientation, bumping into things
- Seizures
- Lethargy, weakness
- Severe bleeding, gaping wound, blood loss
- Profuse, repeated vomiting or diarrhea
- Exposure to poisonous substances, plants, or animals
- Second- or third-degree burns or mild burns covering large areas of the body
- Near-drowning
- Electric shock

how will you transport your pet in an emergency?

Consider how you will transport your dog in an emergency. Many people, especially those living in large cities, rely on taxis, public transportation, or other forms of getting around town. If you don't have a car, plan ahead for how you could transport your dog to the vet in an emergency. Will a taxi driver accept your injured dog in a cab? Do you have a reliable friend nearby or relative who drives? Devising a plan now will give you one less thing to worry about should an emergency arise.

Including Your Dog in Your Family Emergency Plan

Imagine you're asleep upstairs when your house catches fire. Can you and your dog escape from the second-story window? Or severe flooding forces you from your home with only minutes to spare. What steps can you take to protect your dog? What if disaster strikes while you're at work and the roads are closed, preventing you from getting home to rescue your dog?

For these and a hundred other reasons, a household's disaster-preparedness plan must include pets. The steps below maximize a dog's chance of survival and of staying with the family during an evacuation, not to mention being reunited if you become separated.

AT THE FIRST SIGN OF AN APPROACHING DISASTER, BRING YOUR DOG INDOORS.

Many animals hide when they sense danger. Bring your dog indoors and make sure his collar and ID tags are securely fastened. Get his crate and evacuation kit and place them near the door.

ALWAYS TAKE YOUR DOG WITH YOU.

Taking your dog with you in an evacuation might seem like a no-brainer, but many well-meaning people, in their panic, believe their dogs will be able to fend for themselves until they can return home. The truth is there's no way of knowing how long you'll be kept out of the area, and dogs left behind in an emergency can become disoriented, lost, injured, or killed.

CREATE A PET BUDDY SYSTEM.

Make arrangements with two or three trusted neighbors who'd be willing to retrieve your dog if you're not home. Give them a house key, show them where the leash and evacuation kit are, and keep their contact numbers on hand or programmed into your cell phone. If you have an alarm system, be sure they know the security code.

PURCHASE AN EVACUATION HARNESS (if you live in a multistory home or apartment building).

If your only hope of evacuating yourself and your dog is through an upstairs window and you have time to safely do so, a search-and-rescue-style harness or dog life vest might save his life (see Resources, page 157). Depending on which type you buy, you may need to preattach a length of rope and carabiner to the handle to lower your dog to safety. Practice putting it on and make sure the fit and material can support your dog's weight. Then stow it under your bed or somewhere easily accessible. For smaller dogs, a soft crate or doggie tote can be similarly rigged.

GET A FLOAT COAT IF YOU LIVE IN AREAS PRONE TO HURRICANES AND FLOODS.

A brightly colored canine life vest will not only help your dog stay afloat in rising flood waters, it will also make him more visible to rescuers should you become separated. Keep it in or near his evacuation kit so you won't have to search for it in a panic.

APPOINTING A GUARDIAN

What would happen to your dog if you were to die? If you shudder at the very thought of it, you may want to have an official plan. Begin by choosing three suitable guardians who are willing and able to fill your shoes. Why three? People's lifestyles can change, and an illness or new job might render one of your choices unable to accept the responsibility down the road. Once you've confirmed your guardians, write up a letter stating your wishes, include their names and contact info, sign and date it, and attach it to your will, living trust, or other important documents. Be sure to include any special feeding or medical instructions, the number of your vet, microchip information, and so on.

your dog's evacuation kit

Be prepared for a last-minute evacuation with your dog by keeping the following items together in a sturdy duffle bag near your family's own evacuation kit:

- Enough food for at least three days
- Food/water dish
- Extra leash
- Collar and ID tag containing current cell phone number and additional emergency contact (family member or friend)
- Vaccination records
- Microchip information
- Medications
- Photo and written description of your dog (for rescue organizations, in case you become separated)
- Waste bags
- Blanket, bed, toys, and treats

Whenever possible bring your dog's crate and as much drinking water as you can manage (three to five days' worth is ideal).

CHECK FOR "RED FLAG WARNINGS" IF YOU LIVE IN A BRUSH FIRE–PRONE AREA.

If you live in a fire-prone region, bookmark the weather-service Web page for your area and check it daily during fire season. Stay extra mindful on these days if you must leave your dog alone, and take precautions such as filling up additional water bowls around the house in case you are delayed due to a fire in your area.

STAY SAFE DURING A TORNADO.

If you live in a high-risk tornado area, be sure your tornado-safe room or cellar is dog friendly. Store toxic items out of reach and sweep nails or other sharp objects from the floor. Keep a bed, blanket, food, and toys there. Most importantly, make sure your dog is familiar with the room and visits it often. If possible, teach him to go to there on command.

MAKE A LIST OF BOARDING FACILITIES AND PET-FRIENDLY HOTELS OUTSIDE YOUR IMMEDIATE AREA.

Current health regulations prevent most emergency shelters from accepting pets. Know in advance where you can stay if your family or friends can't accommodate you, and keep the list in your evacuation kit.

OBTAIN "PETS INSIDE" DECALS AND PLACE THEM ON YOUR WINDOWS AND DOORS.

These recognizable decals alert rescuers and others of pets that may be trapped inside in need of evacuation. They can be purchased at your local fire department or various online sources (see Resources, page 157).

KEEP YOUR DOG LEASHED OR CRATED AT ALL TIMES, EVEN IN THE CAR.

Under the stress of evacuation, even the most calm, trustworthy dog may panic, try to escape, hide, or even bite.

KEEP MICROCHIP INFORMATION UPDATED.

Have you recently moved or changed phone numbers? Remember to promptly update any new information with your dog's microchip company.

MICROCHIPS AND TATTOOS

While a well-fitting collar with ID tag is essential for all dogs, they can and often do come off if snagged on a bush, fence, or other obstacle a lost dog may encounter. For this reason, microchips and tattoos offer added security. Microchipping is performed in your vet's office and involves a safe, permanent implant, no bigger than a grain of rice, injected between your dog's shoulder blades. The chip carries your contact information and can be read by scanners kept at most animal shelters, rescue organizations, and veterinary clinics. Tattoos are also done by your vet and are usually placed on the dog's inner thigh. (Both processes include an ID tag for your dog to wear that lists the contact information for the registering company.)

two

DOG- AND PUPPY-PROOFING BASICS

Preventable accidents are a leading cause of injury and death in dogs under eight years of age. You can greatly reduce the risk of accidents by taking a holistic approach to dog and puppy proofing—one that not only removes dangerous items from her environment, but also satisfies her natural urges for play, exercise, and socialization to relieve the stress and boredom that can lead to destructive behavior. This section shows you how to incorporate an easy-to-follow dog- and puppy-proofing plan, training tips, and other tricks and strategies to keep your pooch safe and happy—plus a few ideas on how to protect your home from the wear and tear of everyday dog ownership.

Keep in mind that although many of the safety tips in this section are separated into those for "dogs" and those more relevant to "puppies," both apply to canines of all ages—especially those that refuse to mellow with age!

Evaluating Dog-Proofing Needs, Indoors and Out

Successful dog proofing varies from home to home and dog to dog. The key is to pay special attention to your dog's individual characteristics and take extra precautions where necessary. For example, if your dog is food obsessed, secure trash and keep dangerous food items from reach at all times. If she's an escape artist, focus on finding the perfect fencing solution. If your elderly dog is losing her vision or coordination, you might place gates around stairs, raised decks, and swimming pools. And for "mouthy" dogs, remove all choking hazards and toxic substances from her environment. Even if your dog is a model citizen, some level of dog proofing is necessary, as many accidents are the result of simply being in the wrong place at the wrong time.

INSIDE YOUR HOME

Get a Dog's-Eye View. Start by getting down on your hands and knees and consider what life looks like from your dog's point of view. Crawl from room to room and see what trouble you can get yourself into. Which wastebaskets and trash cans can you knock over or put your snout into? What's on the coffee table? What cupboards can you open, and what's lying around on the floor in the kids' room? Remember, you are bored, curious, and easily amused, and you have strong, sharp teeth and an unbelievable sense of smell. Remove or securely store anything toxic, sharp, chewable, or otherwise dangerous (see Part 3, page 52, for a detailed exploration of these items).

This exercise can also be a fun and educational activity to do with your children, as it will teach them about dog-related hazards and how to be a responsible pet owner, all while crawling around on the floor like an animal!

Secure Trash. Many dogs show a keen interest in kitchen garbage—and who could blame them? The kitchen trash is full of enticing food scraps, but it's also home to a plethora of bacteria and toxin-producing molds from spoiled foods, which can cause stomach upset, food poisoning, and at their worst, seizures and other dangerous neurological effects. Other items like poultry bones, plastic wrap, and aluminum foil can cause choking, cuts, or intestinal obstruction. Make sure your kitchen garbage bin is a sturdy one with a tight-fitting lid. If possible, store it under the sink or behind a cabinet.

Wastebaskets in other areas of the home can also draw the attention of curious canines, and often contain hazards like razor blades, dental floss, and discarded medications and toiletries. Take similar precautions with these as well, and keep them in a closed cabinet.

Remove Food Hazards. Many types of "people food" can be dangerous to dogs, including raisins, grapes, chocolate, macadamia nuts, sugar-free gum, onions, and coffee grounds. Make sure everyone in your household knows these food hazards—especially if your dog likes to snitch off plates and counters when no one's looking. See page 56 for a complete list of toxic foods (and a handy guide in Appendix II), and make keeping them out of the dog's reach part of your daily dog-proofing mind-set.

Identify Your Houseplants. They're lovely to look at, but are they safe? Some common houseplants like pothos and aloe can be harmful to nibbling dogs. Refer to the Toxic Plant Guide (page 149) for assistance in avoiding hazardous indoor greenery.

Check Tabletops. You wouldn't think a dog would swallow loose change, but just about every veterinarian has a story about the poodle who thought she was a piggy bank. Some coins, such as pennies minted after 1982, contain high levels of zinc, which can cause kidney damage and other ailments if swallowed. Other tabletop hazards include cigarettes, ashtrays and matches, potpourri and solid air fresheners, chewing gum, and jewelry.

Tidy Up for Safety. Many choking or swallowing hazards are the very items frequently left lying around the house—children's toys and balls, game pieces, yarn, socks, shoelaces, hair ties, and sewing and craft supplies. Office supplies such as paper clips, pens, and staplers are also risky. While we may never know exactly what motivates some dogs to swallow non-food items, we do know it can be avoided by simply putting them away. (To learn more about the most common choking and intestinal obstruction hazards, see page 53.)

Safely Store Vitamins and Medications. Vitamins and medications meant for people, including prenatal vitamins and iron supplements, cold medicines,

acetaminophen, diet pills, and antidepressants, can be very hazardous to dogs. Many coated pills and liquid medicines have a sweet flavor, which makes them an enticing snack—and child-proof caps are no match for sharp canine teeth. Carefully store all pills, medications, inhalers, nicotine patches, and other items in securely closed cabinets or drawers. Never give "people" medications, over-the-counter remedies, or vitamins to your dog without veterinary approval.

Keep Cleaning Supplies Out of Reach. Household cleansers, bleach, drain cleaners, laundry soap, fabric softener sheets, and dishwashing detergent are just some of the household supplies that may contain harsh and caustic agents that can burn, poison, or otherwise injure a dog (or human, for that matter!). To protect your pooch, wipe up spills, close bottles tightly, and store behind high or lockable cabinet doors, and choose nontoxic alternatives whenever possible.

Baby gates are an effective way to confine your dog to safe areas of the home—and thanks to a variety of attractive new designs, they needn't be an eyesore.

safety tips
bolting out the front door

Many dogs will bolt out an open front door because they see it as a rare and exciting opportunity to explore outdoors, or cut loose and burn off pent-up energy. Unfortunately, a dog that bolts can be hit by a car, attacked by another dog, or lost. One way to prevent this is to desensitize your dog to the open door, making it "no big deal." Start exposing your puppy or new dog as early as possible to the door opening and closing. Do it twenty times a day (when there is no traffic or other danger in case she slips by you). Have friends come in and out, knocking and ringing the doorbell, entering and exiting without fanfare. In time, an open front door will become a boring thing to your dog.

Alternatively, use baby gates to create a "dog-safe zone" in your house, blocking off your dog's access to opening doors.

DOGGIE DAMAGE CONTROL:
SCRATCHING AT THE DOOR

Door scratches are a common complaint among dog owners. Fortunately, there are several methods of addressing this problem.

The first and simplest solution is to **install a pet door**. Many trainers agree that dogs are happiest when they can go indoors and outdoors as they please—provided the outdoor area is safely fenced. There are now pet doors available to suit nearly every style: a standard wooden door, a glass slider, French doors, and so on.

Some dogs will scratch at the front door after you've left the house. To prevent door damage, **use self-sticking door covers or protective plastic door shields** (see Resources, page 157, for more information).

Training your dog not to scratch in the first place is optimal. Try attaching a training mat (also known as a Scat Mat) along the area where the dog scratches. These battery-operated plastic sheets or strips discourage scratching by delivering a safe yet uncomfortable static charge when touched by the dog's paws. After the dog realizes that scratching leads to discomfort, you can remove the training mat.

To hide scratches that already exist on your door, **use a commercial scratch remover for wood. You can also use a wax crayon or wood putty pencil** that best matches the door color and work it into the scratch marks, using a hair dryer to soften the wax as needed. After filling in the scratches, buff with a soft cloth.

Note: Some door scratching may be due to separation anxiety. For more on separation anxiety, see page 45.

SAY NO TO RAT BAIT

Rat bait is one of the most dangerous substances a dog can get into. Dog owners should never use these poison pellets—even in places like the attic. If it's anywhere in the home, there's no guarantee it can't wind up somewhere else—especially since rats are known to drag the bait back to their nests, which could be accessible to curious canines. A smarter alternative is to use humane traps, or, if they are in the attic or another area your dog can't access, traditional snap traps or electronic traps.

Unplug Paper Shredders. Paper shredders, often in the home office, can pose a danger to dogs and puppies. Shredders left on "automatic" mode can catch a wagging tail or roving tongue. Although these accidents are rare, keep your paper shredder off the floor, on the desk, turned off, or unplugged when not in use.

IN THE GARAGE AND BACKYARD

Mend Fences. The first step in dog proofing your yard is to make sure the area is securely enclosed. Check your fencing for holes or gaps, and make any necessary repairs to prevent your dog from getting out (and others from getting in). While many dogs are content to stay on their home turf, other restless souls will dig, jump, or wiggle their way out of even the best fences. (For more tips on fencing, see page 77.)

Weed Out Poisonous Plants and Other Garden Hazards. Consult the Toxic Plant Guide on page 149. Some common backyard plants that are extremely dangerous include sago palm and oleander, and even toadstools and some wild mushrooms can cause problems if consumed. Remove anything that might pose a risk to grazing canines.

Compost piles or bins should always be blocked off from pets. The growing popularity of home composting has resulted in an increase of "compost poisoning" caused by the fermentation of meat, dairy products, and other foods—none of which should be in compost bins—that produce clostridial toxins, molds, and bacteria such as salmonella, which can be very harmful to a dog.

Secure Chemicals, Paints, and Automotive Supplies. Scan the garage to see what products are within a dog's reach, and store anything dangerous such as paints, motor oil, turpentine, insecticides, ice-melting products, and swimming pool treatment supplies on high shelves or behind closed cabinet doors. (Detailed information about common hazards found in the garage can be found on page 89.)

Conduct a Ground Inspection. Sweep up nuts, bolts, screws, nails, and other sharp objects that can be harmful if stepped on or swallowed. Check the area under your car for any puddles—only a few licks of dripped motor oil, radiator fluid, or antifreeze can be disastrous (as little as 2 tablespoons [30 ml] of sweet-tasting antifreeze can kill a 20-pound [9 kg] dog!) Store sporting equipment such as golf balls and racquetballs out of reach. In particular, these smaller, slippery balls are choking hazards, and golf balls and paintball pellets can be toxic if swallowed. Finally, make sure large, heavy items such as bicycles, skis, and kayaks are secured so they can't fall over on cavorting canines.

Remove Rodent Traps and Baits. Rodent baits are designed to attract their victims with a sweet taste and smell, which can attract unlucky dogs as well. Check under your house, in garden sheds, and in the corners of your garage for old traps or baits that may have been left by a previous occupant.

Use Caution When Working with Dangerous Equipment or Products. It's great fun to have your dog keep you company while doing home improvement and maintenance projects. But there are certain times when it's best to work solo, like when you're using power tools, lawn mowers, and caustic chemicals—on these occasions, keep her inside so she can't get underfoot and injure you or herself.

safety tip

safe party planning

Many dogs love a good people party and view it as an opportunity to score lots of extra attention, not to mention a jackpot under the hors d'oeuvre table. Other dogs can become overwhelmed by the noise, bustling activity, and influx of strangers into the home. For dogs in the latter category, provide a safe, quiet place for them to stay during the festivities, whether it's an upstairs bedroom, a friend or neighbor's house, or a boarding facility. If you allow your dog to mingle among the guests, be sure all dangerous foods and alcohol are out of reach and that gates are kept closed—and be extra diligent during kids' parties, where the cake spills, the toys fly, and doors are left open in the midst of the collective sugar-induced frenzy!

For dogs with an intense fear of fireworks, consult your veterinarian about a prescription sedative, or consider leaving her with a friend at a quiet location.

DOGS AND FIREWORKS

For many dogs, fireworks are no cause for celebration. The loud noise and vibrations can be so intensely terrifying that with every such holiday or festival, animal shelters are inundated with lost pets who have dug, chewed, and clawed their way out of their homes and yards to run for cover. Other dogs remain inside but injure themselves trying to scratch and burrow their way into closets, through screen doors, and under furniture to hide. If your dog is afraid of fireworks, take care to ensure her sanity and yours by following a few simple guidelines.

Never take your dog with you to the fireworks display—you may think she'll feel safer with you, but it will only bring her closer to the fear-inducing stimulus. Leave her at home, in her crate if possible, with the curtains drawn and windows closed.

Fill a Kong or other durable toy with plenty of treats and surround her with other items of comfort, such as her favorite blanket or clothing with your scent on it. Turn on the television or play soothing music on the radio to help drown out the noise.

Natural calming remedies can also be helpful. You can now buy dog biscuits containing valerian root (a natural sedative) or Bach's Rescue Remedy. For extreme cases, consult your vet about a prescription sedative. Be sure to give whatever remedy you're using at least an hour before fireworks are expected to start so they have time to take effect.

Finally, consider boarding your dog or leaving her with a friend that lives in a quieter location.

DOGGIE DAMAGE CONTROL:

VOMIT ON THE CARPET

Why is it that whenever dogs have to vomit, they head straight for the carpet? We may never know the answer, but at least we know a few tricks to clean up the mess.

When cleanup is necessary, act fast, since stomach acids in vomit can discolor carpet. Use a spoon or the edge of a butter knife to lift solid matter, or try "plucking" it up with paper towels. **Do not attempt to scrub or wipe up the mess!** This will only push the vomit deeper into the carpet fibers.

Next, douse the area with baking soda to absorb the moisture and stain-causing acids. Wait for it to dry completely, then vacuum it up thoroughly. Now you can begin blotting—not wiping—the remaining stain: Mix ½ cup (146 g) salt to 2 quarts (2L) water, and blot the soiled area with a sponge. Rinse the sponge thoroughly between blottings. After sponging, apply a carpet spot remover following the label directions. Rinse with cool water, blot with a towel, and allow the area to dry completely.

Choose Nontoxic Household and Garden Products

So, just how important is choosing the right products for the home and garden? Consider this: On any given day a dog may nibble crumbs off the kitchen floor, romp through the yard, curl up on her favorite rug, lick her paws, and take a nap. At the same time, she also ingested floor cleaner, weed killer, carpet deodorizer . . . and so on. Practically every product used to clean the house or treat the garden will, in some quantity, wind up in a dog's system by way of ingestion, inhalation, or skin contact. Household products are a major source of home toxins—some of which can outright kill a dog if consumed. The easiest strategy is to use as many nontoxic, all-natural products as possible, and even then they must be stored securely out of reach when not in use. And remember, many pet-safe garden products still recommend waiting after application before allowing a pet into the treated area. Always follow the package instructions.

For more natural and economical cleaning alternatives, white vinegar, baking soda, lemon juice, and club soda are impressively effective. Potent cleaning recipes using these kitchen staples can be found in a number of books and on many websites. (See Resources on page 157 for a few recommendations.)

DOG PROOFING AT-A-GLANCE

- **Remove Poisons.** Remove toxic plants. Keep hazardous foods, vitamins, and medications out of reach. Secure household cleansers, paints, antifreeze, and other toxic substances on high shelves or in closed cabinets. Remove all rat bait or snail bait from your property.

- **Remove Choking/Obstruction Hazards.** Keep common choking and obstruction hazards away from your dog. Offenders include bones, balls, rocks, squeakers/nondurable dog toys, toys meant for children or smaller pets, socks, underwear, and panty hose.

- **Secure Trash.** Make trash cans and wastebaskets inaccessible by keeping them in cabinets or in cans with tight-fitting lids. Block access to compost piles.

- **Address Physical Safety.** Repair holes and gaps in fences. Ensure gates close properly. Fence off swimming pools. Take care when using lawn mowers and power tools around pets. Remove rodent traps in accessible areas. Unplug paper shredders when not in use.

- **Take Preventive Measures.** Give your dog plenty of exercise, provide her with a variety of safe chew toys to keep her occupied, and teach her basic safety commands such as "stay," "come," and "leave it."

Extra Precautions for Puppies

When it comes to finding trouble, puppies take top prize. The world is a new and curious place for these fuzzy youngsters, and they are hardwired to learn about all its wonders by sniffing, chewing, investigating, and eating anything that isn't nailed down. Some of the most common accidents for puppies are poisoning, choking, and intestinal obstruction. From obvious temptations such as people food to perplexing objects such as rocks and paper clips, the dangerous items that can find their way into puppy tummies are endless.

Other accidents that are more likely to affect puppies include drowning, falls, and electric cord shock.

But, if this all sounds ominous, take heart. While puppies left to their own devices are certainly prone to accidents, most all of them can be prevented through diligent puppy proofing, proper supervision, and positive, age-appropriate training.

ESSENTIAL PUPPY-PROOFING TACTICS

Secure Electrical Cords. A live electrical cord (such as lamp, telephone, and computer cords), combined with a puppy's desire to chew, can cause serious injuries ranging from mouth burns to heart failure. Some ways to prevent electric cord accidents are using cord protectors (which can be found in computer and electronics stores), unplugging cords when not in use, spraying the cords with bitter spray, or taping them up along the wall.

Eliminate Dangling Objects. Dangling cords from draperies and blinds can be attractive to a playful puppy, so tie the cords up on pegs to prevent pups from becoming caught or strangled. Remove or fold up the corners of dangling tablecloths—if heavy items are on top of the table, these can be pulled down on the puppy. The same goes for long vines from hanging houseplants in pots.

Fence Off the Pool. Fence off or otherwise prevent access to pools, hot tubs, and garden ponds when you're not there to supervise your pup. Not only can drinking chlorinated or algae-containing water wreak havoc on their young tummies, drowning is also a major concern. For more on backyard pool safety, see page 91.

Use Child-Proofing Gadgets. Install latches on low cabinets containing harmful cleansers and chemicals. Use outlet covers on electrical sockets, which can catch their toenails or cause burns if licked. Place baby gates at the top and bottom of stairs until your puppy can safely navigate them without clumsiness. And make sure upper decks, balconies, and other raised areas of your home cannot allow your puppy to fall.

See What's Hiding under the Bed. Look under the beds, sofas, and other furniture and remove any wayward items like buttons, coins, string, safety pins, toys, socks, plastic bags, and candy wrappers.

Remove Temptation. Puppies are well known for pilfering small electronics like remote controls, cell phones, and PDAs. Not only are these items all choking and intestinal obstruction hazards, they also contain batteries, which are highly toxic if swallowed. To protect your belongings and your pooch, store these items safely out of reach. Keep open purses, backpacks, and gym bags zipped up and out of the way, as they contain a wide range of nonconsumable no-nos.

multiple-pet households

If you share your home with more than one pet, be sure to keep toys belonging to puppies, small dogs, and cats away from larger dogs—they can be a choking hazard.

Beware of Reclining Chairs. Reclining chairs that are left open in the "reclining" position can trap a puppy that crawls inside, so be sure these types of chairs are upright when not in use.

Start Training Early. Enroll in a puppy class, buy training books and videos, and do all you can to learn positive training methods to teach your pup "come," "stay," "leave it," "drop it," and other safety-minded commands. Establishing the foundation for good communication with your puppy now will benefit you both for years to come. The whole family should participate in training for consistency. And above all, be patient, diligent, and understanding. The more time, effort, and love you put into your puppy, especially in the first couple years, the greater the chances she will mature into a beautifully behaved dog you can take anywhere without worry.

The Benefits of Crating. Teaching a puppy to be comfortable in her crate is an invaluable safety measure for her and a huge convenience for you. There will be many times you'll want to keep her out of the way for her own protection. You could be doing home repairs, painting a room, or carrying hot food. There could be a natural disaster or unexpected airline flight. No matter what may come up, you'll be able to quickly and easily put her in her crate without any fuss or worry. To make your pup's crate a pleasant, inviting place, **never use a crate as punishment!**

To get her started, begin feeding all meals inside the crate. Place her favorite toys inside, or a shirt with your scent on it. Place the crate in an area of the house with a lot of activity, such as the kitchen, so she still feels like part of the family. Sit on the floor next to her open crate and play with her, tossing her toys inside. Praise her whenever she enters the crate on her own. Then when she's ready, fill a durable toy with a little peanut butter or other treats and place her in the crate with it, closing the door. When introduced properly, most puppies love their crate and think of it as a secure, cozy "den." If you have trouble crate-training your puppy or adult dog, consult a trainer for further advice.

PUPPY PROOFING AT-A-GLANCE

- **Address Chewing Dangers.** Secure electrical cords in cord protectors or unplug when not in use. Look under beds, tables, and sofas for choking hazards. Zip up backpacks and purses. Keep cell phones, remote controls, and other electronic gadgets out of reach.

- **Fence Off the Pool and Other Hazards.** Block access to swimming pools, spas, and ponds unless the pup can be supervised. Use baby gates and other methods to ensure the puppy can't fall from balconies, high decks, and stairs.

- **Eliminate Dangling Objects and Physical Hazards.** Secure cords from draperies and blinds, which are a strangulation hazard. Avoid dangling tablecloths with heavy objects on top of the table. Remove dangling houseplants. Keep reclining chairs in the upright position when not in use.

- **Use Child-Proofing Gadgets.** Install latches on low cabinets housing toxic cleansers and other products. Use outlet covers on exposed outlets. Place baby gates where needed to avoid falls or prevent the pup from wandering into dangerous territory.

- **Commit to Training.** Teach safety commands such as "stay," "come," "down," and "leave it." Train the pup to be comfortable when crated.

DOGGIE DAMAGE CONTROL:
HOUSE-TRAINING ACCIDENTS

For many a puppy and some adult dogs too, mastering peeing and pooping outdoors is a "work in progress." In the meantime, the occasional accident on the carpet is to be expected. While cleaning up the mess requires little effort, it's important to do it properly, as even the slightest odor left behind can attract the dog or other pets back to the area to repeat the incident all over again.

The most important tool in your arsenal is an enzyme cleaner made especially for pet stains, which can be purchased at pet supply stores (buy a big bottle—you'll need it). The enzymes break down the odor-causing proteins in the dog waste, eliminating odor.

First remove any solid waste and thoroughly blot up the urine. A sanitary pad or absorbent paper towels will remove as much wetness as possible. Next, apply the enzyme product **very liberally**—completely saturating the stain. Check the area several hours later and reapply lightly if it's already beginning to dry out— this allows the enzymes plenty of time to soak in and do their job. Then wait for the area to dry completely, which can sometimes take up to a full week (speed the process up with an electric fan if desired). Once dry, follow with your favorite carpet stain remover to get rid of any leftover discoloration (make sure it's safe to use on your carpet). Keep your pets away from the area until it's completely dry.

CHEWING ON FURNITURE

If you have a puppy, you may be all too familiar with chewed table legs. One strategy to curtail this behavior is to spray your wood furniture, electric cords, and other off-limits items with bitter apple, a nontoxic deterrent spray available at pet supply stores. However, be warned that some puppies and dogs actually like the taste of the spray! If this is the case with your pooch, there are many other varieties of deterrent spray you can try. Purchase a few small bottles to use as testers until you find one that works.

The Importance of Play and Exercise

Dogs need daily play and exercise for their health and well-being, and to burn off excess energy. Aside from the obvious benefits, a tired, satisfied, happy dog is far less likely to go looking for trouble. For this reason, giving your dog the regular activity she needs is not only a great way to bond, it's also a vital aspect of dog proofing. In fact, many top trainers believe a lack of proper exercise accounts for most destructive behavior.

And its not just physical exercise that matters— dogs also need outlets for mental and social stimulation, just like people. By way of comparison, consider your typical day: You go to work, run around doing your daily activities, interact with other people, perhaps go to dinner or hit the gym. If it's the weekend, you may go for a bike ride, do errands, go to a party, or see a movie.

Now compare these activities to their doggie equivalents: Did your dog take a nice long walk, hike, or romp with her favorite human? Did she stimulate her mind with a challenging game, toy, or new trick? Did she herd sheep, retrieve ducks, or track a scent through the woods? Did she play with her favorite dog pals? If so, chances are, at the end of the day she'll be curled up in her bed snoring contently, too exhausted to chew up your shoes or surf the kitchen counter.

Many dogs that don't like to fetch tennis balls go crazy for soccer balls and basketballs.

PHYSICAL EXERCISE

All adult dogs need sufficient daily exercise tailored to their age, breed, health, and physical condition. Ask your vet or trainer how much and what type of exercise is right for your dog, then get cracking!

As a general rule, healthy pure and mixed breeds that fall into the sporting, working, herding, or hound categories, along with most terriers, should get a daily total of *at least* one hour—preferably more—of activity such as walking, hiking, a short jog, swimming, fetch, or catch—broken up into two or three sessions throughout the day and evening.

Older dogs, giant breeds, or with those with shorter legs require activities with low impact on their joints, so avoid jumping and running.

Toy and many nonsporting breeds need less physical exercise, and may be content with a moderate walk and indoor games.

Short-nosed breeds, such as pugs and bulldogs, can have difficulty breathing if overworked. They're also more susceptible to heatstroke and should not exert themselves in warm weather.

With all types of dogs, be mindful of the climate whenever you exercise outdoors, carry water on longer outings, and avoid hot or cold temperature extremes.

Do not feed your dog immediately before or after hard exercise, which can cause stomach upset and is a possible contributor to bloat, a life-threatening condition (see Bloat, page 132). And always watch your dog to make sure she's not overdoing it in an effort to keep up with you. Chances are, you will find just the opposite, and your pooch will wear you out.

CHOOSING A BREED THAT'S RIGHT FOR YOU

One of the most important things you can do for your new puppy or dog starts before you ever meet her: deciding what type of dog best matches your lifestyle. Get it right and you're likely to enjoy years of mutually rewarding bliss with your new best friend. Get it wrong and you'll both be left frustrated and unfulfilled. So before you hit the local shelter or check into breeders, be honest:

- Do I have a big yard, or live in a small apartment?
- How much time will I be able to spend exercising my dog?
- Do I live in an especially hot or cold climate?
- Do I foresee a lifestyle change or new living arrangement over the next ten years?
- What are my interests—am I sporty and active, or more of a homebody?

(There are also many "breed selector" websites that can help you choose the type of dog that's right for you.)

Breeds that Need Lots of Exercise	Breeds that Need Less Exercise	Breeds Suited to Cold Climates	Breeds Suited to Warm Climates
Australian cattle dog	Bassett hound	Alaskan malamute	Australian cattle dog
Australian shepherd	Bulldog	Akita	Australian shepherd
Brittany	English toy spaniel	Bernese mountain dog	Basenji
Border collie	French bulldog	Great Pyrenees	Chihuahua
English setter	Great Dane	Keeshond	Italian greyhound
Fox terrier	Irish wolfhound	Newfoundland	Manchester terrier
German shorthaired pointer	Maltese	Samoyed	Rhodesian ridgeback
German shepherd	Papillon	Saint Bernard	Toy Manchester terrier
Golden retriever	Pekingese	Siberian husky	
Irish setter			
Jack Russell terrier			
Labrador retriever			
Weimaraner			
Vizsla			

Special Exercise Needs for Puppies

Puppies have different exercise requirements than adult dogs due to their developing bones, joints, and skeletal system. You should never run or jog with your puppy (beyond a short, playful romp), or engage in any lengthy high-impact activity—especially with large-breed puppies, which are often prone to hip dysplasia, osteochrondrosis, and other developmental conditions that can worsen with excessive stress to the bones and joints. Most of your pup's exercise needs can be met with several energetic play sessions and shorter walks on a leash throughout the day. Adding in a couple of brief training sessions will further tire her out. And although you may be tempted to cuddle and play with your puppy all day, remember she also needs plenty of undisturbed sleep, just as a human baby does. (In fact, it's perfectly normal for a younger puppy to snooze away over half the day.)

SOCIAL INTERACTION

Dogs are pack animals and need social interaction with other dogs at regular intervals. They benefit by just being "out in the world," accompanying their humans on errands and family outings that expose them to new situations, noises, and people. You can satisfy your dog's social needs by taking her to the dog park, hosting play dates with friends' dogs, or letting her burn off some serious energy at a cage-free doggie day-care facility once or twice a week. Just be sure your dog is having fun and is not stressed out or overwhelmed by the presence of too many dogs at once, which is obviously counterproductive to positive socialization (consult a professional trainer if your dog exhibits aggressive or fearful behavior). Find the activities that suit her best and stick with those options. Combined with obedience training and leash etiquette, keeping your dog socially active will make her a good canine citizen and a pleasure to be with wherever you go.

MENTAL STIMULATION

As the highly intelligent creatures they are, dogs can easily become bored and frustrated without daily activity to challenge their minds. Luckily, there are many fun and creative ways to play with your dog that can be integrated into your spare time around the house. Here are a few ideas:

Tricks

Spend ten minutes a day teaching your dog a new trick, or practicing old ones. Use treats, keep it fun, and lavish her with praise when she gets it right. A variety of books, websites, and DVDs can give you all the pointers you need. (For a few suggestions, see the Resources section starting on page 157.)

Games

Try these games or invent your own to match your dog's special interests or talents. The ultimate goal with any game should be bonding, fun, and a little challenge. If your dog doesn't seem to be enjoying herself or won't play along, don't force it.

Hide and Seek. When your dog isn't watching, go to the farthest part of the house and hide in a closet, behind a door, or behind a sofa or chair. Call out your dog's name and "Come!" and let her search the house for you. Praise her when she finds you and give her a treat to up the excitement. If your dog likes squeaky toys, sneak off with a toy and squeak it until she finds you. Then give it to her as a reward for her excellent detective work.

Where's the Cookie? Hide your dog's favorite treat somewhere in the house and the next time you see her looking bored, ask her enthusiastically, "Where's the cookie? Where's the cookie?" Let her run around the house with you searching together for the prize, then eventually lead her close enough so she can find it.

Circus Dog. Hold a hula hoop so that the bottom edge is touching the ground. Toss a treat through and encourage your dog to step through the hoop to get it.

Repeat a few more times, then raise the hoop slightly off the floor and toss a treat through again, gradually raising the hoop higher and higher until your dog is leaping like a gazelle.

Bubble Time. This one is simple: Blow bubbles for your dog (using bubbles made especially for dogs, sold at pet supply stores, or nontoxic children's bubbles.) Watch her leap in the air to try to catch them, and praise her for each successful pop.

Crazy Cardboard Roll. Take the empty cardboard cylinder from a roll of paper towels and talk to your dog through it. Go ahead, ham it up a little, and run around the house to see if she'll chase you. The sound of your distorted voice will drive her wild with curiosity!

Toys

Dog toys have become an art form in recent years, with various brands developing more challenging and durable toys than ever before. From puzzles to treat dispensers to plush toys designed to be ripped apart and put back together again, they provide endless ways to stimulate and entertain. Be sure to supervise your dog with all but the most durable toys, and play along when possible to make it bonding time as well. (See Resources, page 157, for suggestions and ordering information.)

THE WELL-STOCKED TOY BASKET

Providing your dog with her very own basket brimming with fun, interesting toys is not only a great way to spoil her, it's also an important part of successful dog and puppy proofing. The key is to make the toy basket a more interesting draw than the garbage can or the shoes you left next to the sofa. Experiment with different toys to see which ones your pup likes best—balls, chew toys, rope toys, interactive toys—just make sure each one is safe and durable enough for her to play with without supervision. Try hiding treats in some of the toys and sneaking them into the mix. This will help teach your dog that checking her basket can often lead to fun surprises. An added benefit to having a toy basket is that it comes in handy when you want to tidy up quickly and need a place to toss all the dog toys lying around the house!

Try a variety of different games and activities with your dog to discover her favorites—indoors and outdoors.

Canine Sports

Canine sports provide physical, social, and mental stimulation all in one outing. Better still, they can also provide an immensely satisfying outlet for your dog's natural breed-specific instincts. Activities include agility, flyball, flying disc, freestyle, water sports, lure coursing, earthdog, and sheep herding. There is literally something for every type of dog, big or small, pure and mixed breeds alike. To choose the right activity for your dog, consider her age, breed, and physical condition, start slowly, and above all, remember to keep it fun.

FINDING YOUR DOG'S PASSION

Most dogs are naturally gifted in specific activities like swimming or agility, but it's often hard to pigeonhole pooches by their breed or size—they will surprise you with their special talents, or lack thereof! The chart below is a starting point for finding your dog's true passion. If you have a mixed breed, all the better—you may have a multitalented star on your hands.

Agility
Australian shepherd
Belgian sheepdog
Border collie
Miniature schnauzer
Mixed breeds
Papillon
Shetland sheepdog
Standard poodle

Swimming
Flat-coated retriever
Golden retriever
Labrador retriever
Newfoundland
Portuguese water dog

Fetching
Border collie
Chesapeake Bay retriever
German shepherd
Golden retriever
Labrador retriever

Jogging
Dalmatian
Irish setter
Pointer
Rhodesian ridgeback
Vizsla
Weimaraner

Flyball
Australian cattle dog
Border collie
Canaan dog
Jack Russell terrier
Mixed breeds
Shetland sheepdog
Whippet

Tricks and Obedience
Bichon frise
German shepherd
Golden retriever
Labrador retriever
Papillon
Toy poodle

Separation Anxiety and Other Causes of Stress

Many dogs feel secure and comfortable when left alone and are perfectly happy to sleep or play with their toys for hours. But dogs that are stressed or suffer from separation anxiety can be destructive to themselves and your belongings. They may chew at their feet or tail, dig under or jump over the fence, scratch on the door, destroy objects in the home, howl, whine, and act overly excited upon your return. If your dog shows signs of separation anxiety, the following strategies can help her become a more relaxed and happy camper while you're away.

PREPARING/CONDITIONING

Give your dog plenty of exercise before you go. This will help release any pent-up energy that might translate into anxious behavior in your absence. When you're finished exercising and she's tired and resting, wait fifteen to thirty minutes for her to settle, give her a couple of treat-stuffed toys to occupy her, then casually stroll out the door. Don't make a big fuss over saying good-bye—just go. Then drive around the block and come home five or ten minutes later.

Return as casually as you left. Ignore the dog for a few moments while you put away your keys, wallet, and coat. Then give her a low-key greeting. Keep your voice calm and happy. Don't baby her if she's acting overly emotional—this will only reinforce the anxious behavior.

If this exercise works well, repeat it a couple of times per day, gradually extending the duration of your absences to fifteen minutes, a half hour, an hour, and so on. Each time you return home to a calm dog that has behaved well in your absence, reward her good behavior with plenty of attention (after you've settled in) and perhaps a fun activity.

Some dogs with separation anxiety start freaking out the moment you pick up your car keys. If this is the case with your dog, there are two things you can try: one is to pick up your keys, put on your coat, and grab your purse or wallet, then just hang around the house or watch TV—without leaving. Repeating this several times a day can help desensitize the dog to these departure triggers. Another idea is to put your coat, keys, and purse/wallet in your car a couple hours before you leave, or even the night before. Then proceed with leaving her as described above.

EXAMINE THE ENVIRONMENT

Whenever a dog shows signs of stress or anxiety, it's important to examine her environment to make sure this isn't contributing to the problem. One thing many trainers agree on is that a dog should always have access to the house. Ideally, this means having a dog door leading to a safe fenced area of the yard, so she can come and go as she pleases. Dogs that are locked outside in their owners' absence tend to be more stressed than those who have access to their "home environment" near their bed, toys, and the places their human pack mates live.

Similarly, dogs that are locked in a crate for hours can also develop anxiety from confinement. Aside from the short-term crating of puppies for the purpose of house-training, dogs should not be locked in their crates for long periods, especially those prone to stressful behavior. A better scenario is to leave the crate door open so the dog can retreat there by choice, without feeling confined.

Don't leave your dog alone for more than five or six hours. Dogs are social pack animals, and as such, they can feel isolated, stressed, and lonely if left for long periods. Have a friend or dog walker stop by, come home at lunch, or enroll your dog in doggie day care. While you're away, leave the television or radio on to re-create household noise.

With patience and consistency, separation anxiety can be greatly reduced in many dogs. The amount of time it takes varies from dog to dog, and some dogs, such as rescues (who often have very justifiable fears of abandonment), require extra care. Consulting a professional trainer or behaviorist is often the best course of action for dogs with extreme separation anxiety. As a last resort, consult your veterinarian about anxiety medication.

Keeping Toy Breeds Safe

Toy breeds require extra diligence where safety is concerned. While larger dogs can withstand falling off the bed or being tripped over, these common mishaps can seriously hurt or even kill a toy breed. The following guidelines can help to protect your pint-size pup.

Keep Her Off High Furniture. Many toy breeds injure themselves falling off furniture. To prevent this, give your dog her own fluffy bed on the floor in your bedroom. Do not let her sleep up on the bed with you. If you absolutely can't follow this rule, at the very least be sure the floor is carpeted and the bed is as low to the ground as possible, and place pet stairs next to the bed (sold at pet supply stores).

Elsewhere in the house, don't let your dog on any high furniture she can't climb down from herself—unless you are holding her carefully. Allow children to hold the dog only while seated on the floor.

Walk This Way. Use a body harness instead of a neck collar on your daily walks. Toy breeds have very delicate necks, and the trachea can be injured by the tension of standard neck collars. When walking through tall grass, gardens, or brush, check that your dog's eyes are protected from thorns, foxtails, and other sharp objects.

Keep Track of Her Whereabouts. Keep an eye on your dog around the house, especially when visitors are present. Toy dogs can be accidentally tripped over and even sat upon. Outside, use caution in places that may have coyotes and other wild predators—some wild animals near suburban areas become so brazen they'll attempt to attack a small dog despite the presence of a human.

Supervise Play. A toy breed can suffer broken bones if roughhousing goes too far while playing with children or larger pets. Teach children how to gently handle the dog, and supervise play between the other furry members of your household.

Use Crates and Carriers for Safety. Provide your dog with a comfortable, properly sized crate and teach her to be content while confined. There will be times you'll need to crate her to keep her away from hazardous activity in the home, such as home repairs, parties, and other occasions when she might get underfoot. In the car, always use a secured pet carrier, seat-belt harness, or small dog car seat.

Say Yes to Sweaters. More so than hardier breeds, toys need extra protection in frigid weather to help prevent hypothermia. So go ahead and buy (or make) that fancy sweater, and she can strut her stuff without shivering.

SAFETY STORY: Mini's Mighty Fall

Mini was an unusually small Chihuahua puppy, and I made a conscious effort to be incredibly careful with her fragile little body. But I wasn't careful enough.

When she was only four months old, I made the mistake of carrying her in my arms with our other older Chihuahua, Tiny. Tiny and Mini "had words" while they were both in my arms and I could not hold them properly as they "wrestled." In slow motion I watched as a helpless little puppy tumbled out of my arms onto the slate floor. Mini suffered a serious concussion and according to the vet was lucky to have survived. It was a horrifying incident.

After that experience we instituted a rule of holding only one dog at a time and we required the "holder" to be seated—preferably on the floor.

But that didn't prevent Mini's next fall: She was on a sofa next to me, playfully bouncing around. She was all by herself (no other dog nearby) and about two feet away from me when she simply took a wrong step and slipped off the couch onto the hardwood floor. I was shocked when I looked down and saw her totally motionless. I wasn't sure if she was even alive at that point. After several long minutes, she came to, slowly, and was raced to the vet clinic. Once again, Mini had gotten a very serious concussion and was lucky to have survived.

We've since made sure to be extra careful with Mini and have pillows or a throw below the couch when she is on it. Interestingly, another Chihuahua we have, Pinky, jumps off the same couch from which Mini fell with ease. Pinky exhibits much greater athleticism than Mini. We truly have to cater to the safety needs of each individual dog. But it's always best to err on the side of caution. I am so grateful to still have Mini 'with us' after her unexpected brushes with death—and hard floors.

—T. Bell, London, U.K.

DOGGIE DAMAGE CONTROL:
DOG HAIR ON UPHOLSTERY

There are many ways to remove those stubborn remnants of dog hair the vacuum leaves behind.

- Use rubber gloves or cloth gardening gloves with nubs on the fingers and palms. Wearing the gloves, whisk your hands briskly across the area, remove the hair from the glove, then repeat until all the hair has been removed.

- A slightly damp kitchen sponge or used fabric softener sheet also removes pet hair well. For those hard-to-reach corners and crevices, wrap tape around your fingers or use a lint brush.

- To discourage your dog from lounging on the furniture altogether, try a training mat (such as a Scat Mat, available at pet supply stores). These transparent, battery-operated plastic mats deliver a safe yet uncomfortable static charge on contact. Lay the mats across the furniture and in time, she'll learn to stay off that velvet armchair and the mats can be removed.

Dogs and Children

Children under ten are the most common victims of serious dog bites, and the majority of these bites are not from strange, vicious dogs running loose in the streets. Most bites happen in the home or another familiar setting with a known, otherwise gentle dog that has been unintentionally provoked. Conversely, children can also injure dogs. So for everyone's protection, children should be taught how to safely interact with all dogs. Also, observe your dog's own tolerance and comfort with children. The following guidelines can help.

Supervise Contact. Monitor the interactions between your child and dog until you can fully trust both of them together. If you sense your dog is uncomfortable around children, don't push it. Consult a trainer for advice.

Teach Proper Play and Petting. Show your child the proper way to pet a friendly dog: by gently stroking or scratching her under the chin, on the chest, or along her body. Teach your child to avoid reaching over the dog's head or patting them on the head, which makes some dogs uncomfortable.

Dogs and babies make an adorable combination—but even trustworthy dogs should be supervised around babies this young.

Teach kids the following "Doggie Don'ts":

- Don't disturb the dog when she is eating, sleeping, or in pain.
- Don't yell, scream, hit, kick, tease, or lunge at the dog.
- Don't take away the dog's bone or toys.
- Don't poke the dog's eyes or ears, or pull her tail.
- Don't feed the dog "people food" or anything else without asking.
- Don't play or lie down in the dog's bed.

Provide a Quiet Place for Your Dog. Dogs need a private area of their own that is off-limits to the kids, such as a crate, bed, or quiet corner of a room. This is a safe place for dogs to retreat from the noise and commotion of children's rambunctious activity when they're feeling overwhelmed.

Educate Kids about "Strange Dogs." Start by teaching them that a strange dog is any dog they're not certain is friendly, or any dog belonging to someone they don't know. Explain the importance of behaving differently around these dogs, since some of them might not be as nice as their own. (See tip box at right.)

ADVICE FOR CHILDREN ABOUT INTERACTING WITH "STRANGE DOGS"

- Always ask permission before petting a strange dog. Then, extend your hand with your palm down to let the dog sniff before petting under the chin.

- Do not look a strange dog directly in the eyes.

- Never run away from a strange dog—instead, stand still with your arms at your sides. If you are knocked down, curl into a ball and cover your face.

- Older children can be taught to recognize the signs of an aggressive dog: growling, snarling, barking with teeth bared, hackles up, snapping, lunging, or raising the tail when approached.

three

HAZARDS IN YOUR HOME

By now you're well aware that the average home contains its share of hazards for dogs and puppies. Now here comes the tricky part: Elaborating on these hazards—such as choking, intestinal obstruction, and household poisons—without turning you into a nervous wreck! This chapter explores common types of accidents and how they happen, to help you prevent them from happening to your own pooch. By learning a little more about this subject, you'll find there is very little actual "work" involved in keeping your dog safe—it will soon come naturally.

Choking and Intestinal Obstruction

Dogs use their mouths constantly: They fetch balls, play with their toys, gnaw on bones, chew sticks, and pick up strange, interesting items they find around the house. Not surprisingly, at times these things can become stuck in their throats or swallowed, both of which can cause serious, life-threatening situations.

Choking occurs when a ball, bone, or other object lodges in the throat and either partially or totally cuts off the dog's air supply. This requires immediate first aid (see Choking, page 134). More common is intestinal obstruction, which occurs when the dog swallows an indigestible object. Often these objects pass through the gastrointestinal tract without incident. However, sharp items like rocks or bone shards can cause tears and lacerations, leading to infection. String or dental floss can literally wrap around the intestines and bind them, and expandable items like sponges or bread dough can swell in the stomach and cause a total blockage, cutting off blood supply to the bowel.

EVERYDAY CHOKING/OBSTRUCTION HAZARDS

Dogs can be indiscriminate in the types of things they swallow. Any item you can hold in your fist is a potential choking or intestinal obstruction hazard. Here is a sample of some of the things vets have removed from dogs' mouths, throats, and digestive tracts:

Baby bottle nipples and pacifiers

Balls (racquetballs, handballs, golf balls, and rubber "superballs" are most common)

Bones/bone shards (cooked and raw)

Buttons

Candy and food wrappers

Chewed-off pieces of dog toys

Clothing items such as socks, underwear, and panty hose

Coins

Corn cobs/corn silks

Diapers (dirty and clean)

Electronics—cell phones, MP3 players, remote controls

Fishhooks

Game pieces and small children's toys

Jewelry

Marbles, jacks, and small plastic figurines

Rawhide or pig ears

Refrigerator magnets

Rocks

Safety pins, paper clips, needles, tacks

Sewing and craft supplies

Shoelaces

Sponges

Squeakers from plush toys (Always supervise dogs that like to rip apart their plush squeaky toys to ensure they don't swallow the stuffing and/or squeaker.)

Sticks

String: meat-wrapping string, yarn, dental floss, ribbon

Tampons and other sanitary supplies

safety tips

signs of choking

It's hard to miss the signs of choking, since the dog will clearly be in distress. Take action immediately! (See Choking on page 134.)

Signs: Dog cannot breathe; struggling or gasping for breath; loud breathing noises; pale, white, or blue gum color; anxiousness or panic; pawing at mouth

signs of intestinal obstruction

The signs of intestinal obstruction may not be visible for days or even weeks and will vary with the location and severity of the obstruction. If you suspect your dog has swallowed something and is showing any of the following signs, seek veterinary treatment immediately.

Signs: Vomiting, diarrhea, loss of appetite, lethargy, depression, weakness, abdominal pain and/or distention, fever or subnormal body temperature, dehydration, shock

SAFETY STORY: Gus's Strange Craving

Gus is my Bernese mountain dog. Since he's the first dog I've had as an adult, it wouldn't be wrong to say I was very "motherly" and watched him like a hawk. But one time when he was nine months old, I put my parents on babysitter duty while I was away on business. After a few days they noticed he wasn't eating or acting like his normal, energetic self, so they took him to the vet … where an x-ray revealed he had swallowed a six-inch (15.2 cm) nylon sock! After some searching, it was determined that he obtained this sock from under the bed, stuffed inside one of my mother's tennis shoes. Poor Gus had to undergo surgery to remove the sock before the blockage created a very serious situation. But thankfully, he made a full recovery. Needless to say, we don't keep anything on the floor anymore.

—*Julene Stelmak, Spokane, Washington*

Everyday Poison Hazards

Each year, thousands of dogs and puppies are accidentally poisoned in their own homes. This most commonly happens when a dog ingests something with an appealing taste or smell (appealing to the *dog*, that is!) such as chocolate, flavored human medications, rodent baits, and other toxic items that they happen to sniff out in their daily wanderings in and around the house.

Dogs can also be exposed to **topical poisonings** when they walk through spilled chemicals or harsh cleansers, such as bleach or pine cleaner, or if a caustic substance is accidentally spilled on their fur.

Inhalation poisoning comes from exposure to carbon monoxide, smoke, fumes from chemical sprays such as pesticides, or chlorine and ammonia gas fumes from household or industrial cleansers. These are far less common than other types of poisonings, but just as serious.

signs of poisoning

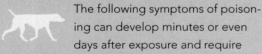

The following symptoms of poisoning can develop minutes or even days after exposure and require immediate action. See Poisoning on page 144 in the Emergency First Aid section and call your veterinarian or poison hotline immediately if you think your dog has been poisoned.

Signs: vomiting or diarrhea; seizures, twitching, trembling, depression, drowsiness, or coma; drooling or foaming at the mouth; coughing heavily; red, blue, gray, or pale gum color (normal color is pink); "drunken" behavior, stumbling, or uncoordination; swollen, red, or irritated eyes; ulcers or burns in or on mouth, lips, or skin; bleeding from mouth, nose, or anus.

TOXIC FOODS FOR DOGS TO AVOID

When it comes to toxic foods, the level of danger is determined by the individual dog and the quantity consumed. Some dogs can eat an entire bag of raisins with no reaction whatsoever, while others might suffer acute kidney failure from even a modest quantity. The safest thing to do is prevent your dog from consuming any of the food items listed below.

Alcoholic Drinks

Alcohol poisoning in dogs can result in vomiting, diarrhea, clumsiness, central nervous system depression, tremors, coma, and even death. Do not leave drink glasses unattended around a curious dog, and be extra careful during parties in your home.

Avocado

The flesh, pits, and skin of avocados contain a toxin known as persin, which can cause vomiting and diarrhea in dogs. The pits are not only toxic, but they also pose a choking hazard.

Chocolate

The higher the cocoa content, the higher the risk. Baker's or dark chocolate is high, whereas milk chocolate is much lower. Ingestion of any type of chocolate, depending on the quantity consumed, can cause drooling, vomiting, diarrhea, hyperactivity, muscle tremors, seizures, and coma. For example, a 3-ounce (85 g) chunk of dark chocolate is enough to be fatal to a 25-pound (11 kg) dog.

Coffee/Coffee Grounds

Caffeine toxicity is similar to chocolate toxicity and can cause the same serious problems.

Fruit Seeds and Pits (pips)

Apples, cherries, peaches, and similar fruits contain cyanide in their seeds, pits, leaves, and stems and can cause varying degrees of illness if consumed in moderate to large quantities. The actual fruit flesh has not been reported to cause harm. The peels, fruit, and seeds of citrus fruits such as lemons and oranges contain citric acid, limonin, and volatile oils, which can cause gastrointestinal upset, vomiting, diarrhea, and central nervous system depression if consumed in large quantities.

Garlic (large quantities)

See "Onions." While included in many dog treats and foods at safe levels, large quantities of garlic can cause a similar reaction to that of onions.

Grapes

Grapes and raisins can be highly dangerous to some dogs, although thus far the veterinary community has yet to discover exactly why. Some signs of grape poisoning are vomiting, loss of appetite, lethargy, abdominal pain, and the possibility of acute kidney failure.

High-Fat Foods

Large quantities of steak trimmings, turkey skin, bacon fat, and other high-fat foods like gravy can cause problems ranging from gastrointestinal upset to pancreatitis, a life-threatening illness. The effects can be cumulative from regular feeding, or acute from one large serving.

Hops

Ingestion of hops, found in home beer-brewing kits, can cause malignant hyperthermia—an uncontrollable fever—which can be fatal.

Macadamia Nuts

Even a few ounces (or grams) of macadamia nuts can cause vomiting, weakness, depression, tremors, and temporary paralysis of the hind legs. Symptoms usually resolve themselves in a few days, unless complicated by other pre-existing medical conditions.

Moldy Food/Trash

Moldy foods often found in trash cans can contain mycotoxins, which when consumed can cause acute vomiting, tremors, and other central nervous system disorders. Spoiled foods can also harbor harmful bacteria such as salmonella.

Onions, Chives, and Onion Powder

When onions are broken down in the digestive system, they can cause damage to red blood cells, causing anemia (low red blood cell count). Dogs that are severely affected may require blood transfusions or oxygen therapy.

Raisins (sultanas)

See "Grapes."

Salt

Salt and foods containing large quantities of salt can produce sodium poisoning, which causes vomiting, diarrhea, excessive thirst, depression, tremors, elevated body temperature, and seizures.

Tea and Tea Bags (caffeinated)

See "Chocolate" and "Coffee/Coffee Grounds."

Xylitol (a common sugar substitute)

Products such as chewing gum, mints, candy, baked goods, and diabetic products are often sweetened with xylitol, which when ingested by dogs can cause a sudden drop in blood sugar, resulting in depression, loss of coordination, and seizures. To date, there have been no reports of problems with other sweeteners.

Yeast Dough

Once ingested, uncooked yeast dough for bread, rolls, and other baked goods can literally "rise" in a dog's stomach and cause blockage in the digestive tract. In addition, as the yeast rises, the alcohol produced during the fermentation process can cause alcohol poisoning.

Kibble Wisdom: Protecting Your Dog from Contaminated Food

Most dog food manufacturers go to great lengths to ensure their products are safe, from inspection and testing of raw ingredients, to date coding and batch testing the final product. Despite these precautions, on rare occasions dry dog food can become tainted with harmful toxins and other contaminants that can sicken or even kill pets. The product is recalled, word spreads like wildfire, and dog owners are left to worry and wonder what they can do to ensure the safety of their own dog's food.

From a logical standpoint, smaller pet food companies have smaller quantities of product to police than mega-manufacturers. They're also more likely to include a customer service telephone number and website on their packaging, and be more willing to disclose their ingredient sources, nutritional information, and food safety practices. When choosing a brand of dog food, try contacting the company up front to see how willing they are to share information—it could make a big difference in the future if there's ever a problem with the food. Also look for packaging that includes clear batch numbers for identification and expiration dates to ensure freshness.

If your chosen pet food company keeps an email list for promotional mailings, consider joining it. You may receive a few unwanted messages, but you'll also receive notice should a recall occur. National humane societies and animal welfare organizations are usually also among the first to display recalled food reports on their websites. Stay informed by checking these periodically.

FOLLOW SAFE STORAGE AND FEEDING GUIDELINES

Dry food must be stored properly to prevent spoilage. First, food should be stored in a moisture-free environment, preferably in temperatures below 75°F (23.8°C) to prevent the growth of toxic mold.

Kibble should be stored in its original packaging in an airtight container. Alternatively, the open bag should be secured with a strong clip between feedings. Resist the urge to store loose kibble in a large plastic bin or trashcan. Most dry foods contain fats whose residue can turn rancid and contaminate the next batch of food. Also, unless a storage container is designated as food grade, harmful chemicals used in manufacturing can leach into the food. Storing the kibble in its own bag in an airtight container will also help keep track of expiration dates, batch numbers, or UPC code for later reference.

Try to purchase food in smaller quantities whenever possible so you have the best chance that the final serving will be as nutritious as the first. Repeated exposure to light and air can degrade a food's nutrients.

Avoid feeding two different types of commercial food at once—if there's ever a problem, you won't know which food is the culprit. And finally, never feed your dog food that smells "off" or looks different than it normally does.

KNOW THE WARNING SIGNS

Signs a dog may exhibit after eating tainted food include vomiting, diarrhea, lethargy, excessive thirst, excessive urination, dehydration, and loss of appetite. If your dog shows any of these signs, or suddenly rejects a food he normally eats with enthusiasm, stop feeding the food, take him to the vet immediately and contact the company to report the problem.

CHOOSING TREATS AND CHEWS

They are in every pet store: glorious bins of dried, smoked animal parts—rawhide, cow hooves, and pig ears, snouts, and tails. You know how much your dog would love to wrap her paws around one of them and devour it with delight. Sadly, you should resist the urge to fill your shopping cart with these tasty chews. **Rawhide and other dried animal parts can cause choking, intestinal blockage, lacerations, and even bowel perforation**—life-threatening injuries requiring emergency treatment. Dogs tend to devour them with such enthusiasm, they bite off and swallow large, sharp chunks, which are very slow to digest and can swell and scrape their way through the gastrointestinal tract. When choosing a longer-lasting style chew for your dog, stick with those labeled as highly digestible, such as starch-based edible chews. And even with nonaggressive chewers, supervise your dog while she enjoys these types of treats, taking care not to let her swallow any big chunks.

Luckily, most pet stores also carry a variety of safe, natural cookie-style treats. When making a selection, remember the fewer ingredients, the better. Look for meat, whole grains, fruit, vegetables, and natural preservatives such as mixed tocopherols. Many types of fresh foods also make safe and nutritious treats for dogs. If your dog isn't used to eating fresh food, start by giving him just a little until you see how he does with it—some dogs have very sensitive stomachs and certain things may not agree with them. Also, although fresh food is excellent for your dog's health (especially a completely home-cooked diet), **do not allow these treats, or any commercial dog treats, to make up more than 10 percent of your dog's total daily food intake.** Exceeding this limit once in a while is fine—but over the long term, it could interfere with the nutrient balance of your dog's diet (not to mention cause unhealthy weight gain). If you find your dog loves fresh food and you decide to take the plunge into home cooking, there are now a variety of reputable books, websites, and services that can help you prepare balanced meals for long-term feeding (see Resources, page 157, for more info).

Nonaggressive chewers can enjoy a beef femur bone once in a while…provided you're willing to supervise the activity to ensure the bone doesn't crack or splinter.

SAFE FOOD TREATS

Banana

Apple slices

Carrots, steamed or raw, cut into bite-size pieces

Plain yogurt

Cooked chicken, turkey, salmon, liver, or other meat (avoid skin, fat, and seasonings)

Steamed green beans

Hard-boiled egg

Sardines (bones and skin are fine here)

Peanut or almond butter

Canned plain pumpkin or cooked butternut squash

Blueberries

Baked sweet potato

RECIPES FOR HOME-BAKED TREATS

These treats are packed with nutrients such as omega-3 fatty acids and vitamin D (from salmon) and calcium carbonate (from dried eggshell). Feed one medium or two small salmon treats a day and your dog will thank you with lots of fishy kisses. These two recipes are courtesy of Catherine Lane of The Possible Canine in Rupert, Quebec.

Wheat-Free Salmon Treats

Ingredients
8 ounces (226 g) cooked fresh or canned wild salmon with juice, no salt

½ cup (30 g) finely chopped fresh parsley

3 whole eggs, preferably organic, beaten well

½ cup (72 g) finely ground sesame seeds (use a clean coffee grinder and make sure there are no traces of coffee grounds in it)

2½ cups (395 g) brown or regular rice flour (or potato, amaranth, quinoa, or chestnut flour)

1 finely ground dried eggshell, preferably organic

To dry the eggshell, save the empty shell of an organic egg, rinse thoroughly, and allow to air-dry completely. Place on a baking sheet and bake for 10 minutes at 300°F (150°C, gas mark 2). Grind the dried shell into a fine powder in a *clean* coffee grinder or with an herb grinder. You can bake many shells at once and store the eggshell powder in an airtight container in the refrigerator. One eggshell is the equivalent of 1 scant teaspoon.

Preheat oven to 375°F (190°C, gas mark 5). Mix all of the ingredients together thoroughly by hand or in a food processor. When the dough is a good consistency for rolling (add a little water or more flour if necessary to avoid sticking), roll out the dough to about ¼ inch (0.6 cm) thick. Use cookie cutters to cut various shapes, or make small patties by hand. Lay cookies out on parchment-lined baking pans and bake for 25 minutes. Cool before serving. Refrigerate a week's supply and freeze the rest for later use.

Note: To make these treats extra nutritious, you can also add ¼ cup (70 g) finely ground raw, plain pumpkin seed or 1 teaspoon of dried alfalfa to the dough before baking.

Turkey Loaf

While not "nutritionally complete and balanced" for long-term feeding, this dish is gluten free, offers excellent protein content, and can be used as a special-day supper or nutritious, high-quality treat in place of cookies.

Ingredients
2 pounds (907 g) ground turkey
½ cup (113 g) cooked, mashed sweet potato
½ teaspoon minced fresh garlic
1 egg, beaten
2½ cups (488 g) well-cooked brown rice
Fresh minced parsley (optional)
½ cup (118 ml) homemade turkey or chicken stock (no onion, no salt, fat skimmed)

Preheat oven to 350°F (180°C, gas mark 4). Grease a 9-inch (23 cm) loaf pan; set aside. In a large mixing bowl, combine the ground turkey, sweet potato, garlic, egg, rice, and parsley, if using. Mix together well and press into the prepared loaf pan. Flatten the mixture, then use a table knife to cut a few shallow slits on top. Pour the stock over the loaf and bake for 1 to 1¼ hours or until nicely browned on top. Cool, then cut the loaf into about 6 slices. Wrap in foil and store in the refrigerator, or freeze for later use. To serve, either use the slices for a meal or break into bite-size pieces for treats.

Many types of "people food" make safe, nutritious snacks for dogs. You may be surprised at what your dog enjoys. Carrots? Bring 'em on!

TOXIC SUBSTANCES AROUND THE HOUSE

You wouldn't expect a dog to eat the contents of an ashtray or old mothballs. But human logic doesn't apply to curious puppies, or dogs with indiscriminate eating habits! The items listed below can all pose a danger to dogs, so be sure to keep them well out of reach, and call your veterinarian or Poison Control Center if your dog has eaten or been otherwise exposed to a toxic substance.

Acetaminophen, such as Tylenol and Excedrin

Antidiarrhea products like Lomotil and Imodium

Aspirin

Batteries, all kinds, typically found in remote controls, watches, hearing aids, and toys

Bleach

Breath strips

Citrus-based cleansers

Diet pills

Essential oils such as lemon, tea tree, eucalyptus

Fabric softener sheets

Glues, especially strong-hold or expanding glue products

Homemade play dough or modeling clay

Household cleansers such as ammonia, dishwashing and laundry detergent, drain cleaner, and furniture polish

Ibuprofen/NSAIDS such as Aleve, Advil, Nuprin, Motrin, or Vick's NyQuil

Lead items (old paint, drapery weights, wine-bottle cork foils)

Marijuana, cocaine, and recreational drugs

Matches

Mothballs

Mouthwash

Pennies (U.S.) minted after 1982 (due to high zinc content)

Phenol-based cleaners like Lysol or Pine-Sol

Potpourri, especially liquid potpourri

Prenatal and other human vitamins, especially high-iron formulations

Prescription medications such as antidepressants, birth control pills, painkillers, and other opiates

Rat and mouse bait-traps and rodent-control products

Rubbing alcohol

Tobacco and nicotine products such as snuff, nicotine gum, cigarette butts, cigars, transdermal patches, and more

myth busters: silica gel packets

You've seen them in bags of dog treats, vitamin bottles, and various packaged foods—those little packets stamped DESSICANT: DO NOT EAT! These tiny fear-provoking pouches are filled with silica gel, a substance used to absorb moisture and increase a product's shelf life. And while it's true they are not meant for human or canine consumption, one or two of these packets should not be harmful if accidentally consumed by your dog.

Create a dog-friendly laundry room by storing dangerous items such as detergent, bleach, and fabric softener sheets safely out of reach.

CHOOSING THE SAFEST FLEA AND TICK CONTROL PRODUCTS

Pesticides used in some flea and tick control products may pose a health risk to pets—especially those containing organophosphates or carbamates, which are still found in several over-the-counter brands. Overexposure and misuse of these products can be toxic to dogs (cats are even more susceptible). Generally, flea and tick control products sold at your veterinarian's office are safer. These include "spot-on" products, and others containing insect growth regulators (which are not pesticides, but instead work to stop the development of young fleas). Consult your veterinarian for recommendations, follow label instructions carefully, and remember to never combine products (i.e., bathing your dog with flea shampoo and then putting on a flea collar) without a vet's approval. While any flea product can harm your dog if used incorrectly, these safer alternatives offer protection against fleas and ticks with far less worry.

A WARNING ABOUT "HUMAN" MEDICATIONS

Never give human painkillers (such as acetaminophen, ibuprofen, or aspirin) to your dog to relieve pain. Even in modest doses, these pain relievers can cause intestinal or kidney damage in dogs. Countless other prescription and over-the-counter drugs, diet pills, recreational drugs, cold medicines, and even certain vitamins can cause serious consequences if ingested by canines. While it's true your veterinarian may sometimes prescribe buffered aspirin, Benadryl (diphenhydramine) Pepcid (famotidine), or other human remedies for your dog, these should only be given with a veterinarian's approval, since considerations such as your dog's weight, age, and state of health will determine the safe, effective dose.

Provide your dog with plenty of safe chew toys in various shapes and textures to help keep him occupied—and to discourage him from seeking out inappropriate items around the house.

SAFETY STORY: The Misadventures of Peggy Sue

Since we rescued our pointer mix Peggy Sue last summer, she has eaten many strange things—a GPS unit, an MP3 player, sunglasses, a loaf of bread, and even once, six whole bananas, peels and all! With each incident we'd step up our efforts to leave nothing dangerous lying around the house, and tried to be careful to make sure all our medications have a child-proof cap and are put away. But one day, Peggy Sue got hold of my hormone pills, chewing through the plastic bottle and safety cap. She had eaten several pills by the time I caught her. I immediately called the vet, who instructed me how to use hydrogen peroxide to make her vomit. She was not too keen on that, but I managed to give it to her and a minute later, I watched her vomit up the pills with great relief! The moral of the story is, be extremely careful to keep all medications out of reach, and always keep hydrogen peroxide in your cupboard.

—*Jayne Levant, Santa Fe, New Mexico*

The Dangers of Canine Bloat

Canine bloat (also known as gastric dilatation-volvulus or gastric torsion) is a life-threatening condition in which a dog's stomach twists or rotates, causing air, gas, and/or food to become trapped inside it, which the dog is unable to expel by normal channels (belching, vomiting, or flatulence). The blood supply to the stomach and other surrounding organs becomes choked off, requiring immediate emergency treatment. Bloat has a high fatality rate, so it's important for dog owners to know its symptoms and act quickly. A dog can die within hours of becoming symptomatic.

Although bloat can happen to any dog, statistics show that large, deep-chested breeds such as Great Danes and Doberman pinschers are at greater risk. **The first and most important priority for any dog with signs of bloat is to get veterinary help as soon as possible. Signs include unproductive vomiting, pacing, restlessness, and a painful, distended abdomen.**

For more on the signs of bloat and treatment options, see page 132.

Unfortunately, the exact cause of bloat is unknown; therefore it can't truly be prevented. Still, most veterinarians agree that following certain practices, especially with risk-prone breeds, makes good sense.

FACTORS THAT MAY DECREASE THE RISK OF BLOAT

- Dividing daily feeding into two or more meals
- Including canned or fresh food in the diet
- Restricting heavy food and water intake at least one hour before and after exercise
- Dogs that are generally happy and stress free

Breeds prone to bloat, such as the Weimaraner, should be allowed to rest about an hour after eating before engaging in heavy exercise.

safety tip:
preventive surgery for bloat

A surgical procedure called gastropexy can help prevent stomach torsion, the most deadly aspect of bloat. This procedure, which can now be performed laparoscopically, involves tacking the side of the stomach wall to the body wall, to prevent the stomach from rotating. Many veterinarians believe bloat can be avoided with gastropexy, and recommend it for high-risk breeds such as Saint Bernards, Great Danes, and other deep-chested breeds. You could have it done at the same time you spay or neuter your dog, or schedule it as a stand-alone procedure. If you have an at-risk breed, consider speaking with your veterinarian about this potentially life-saving preventive measure—especially if you live more than a half hour away from a veterinary hospital.

Dividing a dog's daily ration of food into two or more feedings may help reduce the risk of bloat.

FACTORS THAT MAY INCREASE THE RISK OF BLOAT

- Feeding only one meal per day
- Gulping down food or gorging on large quantities of food
- Previous history of bloat, or dog has family history of bloat
- Senior-age dogs tend to bloat more frequently
- Dogs that are anxious, fearful, or aggressive tend to bloat more often
- Male dogs tend to bloat more often than females

Electric Cord Shock

Electric cord shock is a potentially life-threatening emergency that happens when a puppy or dog chews through the protective coating of a live electric cord. Although any chew-happy dog is at risk, puppies' natural curiosity, needle-sharp teeth, and strong desire to chew make them a magnet for lamp, computer, and telephone cords.

In a mild case of electric shock, electric current reacts with the puppy's wet mucous membranes, causing burns to the lips, tongue, and mouth. The puppy will cry out loudly in pain and may be unable to unclamp his teeth from the cord. In more severe cases, electric current runs through the whole body, causing injuries such as circulatory distress, seizures, lung damage, collapse, and even death.

In any instance of electric shock, **the first thing you must do is disconnect the power at the main circuit breaker.** Your natural reaction will be to rush to your puppy's aid, but you mustn't touch him until the power is disconnected or you could be electrocuted, too. Once the main circuit breaker has been turned off, unplug the cord. If you can't get to the breaker fast enough, look for a nonconductive item like a wooden chair or broomstick to move the pup away from the cord, or unplug the cord with a rubber glove.

If you ever come home and smell an odor of burning flesh or fur from your dog, check his mouth for any blackened or burn marks, and check electric cords for bite marks.

TIPS FOR PREVENTING ELECTRIC CORD SHOCK

- Unplug cords when not in use.
- Tape up cords or place them in inaccessible locations.
- Spray accessible cords with bitter spray repellent (available at pet supply stores).
- Buy cord covers (or cord protectors) at hardware, computer, or electronics stores.
- Inspect cords periodically for bite marks, and if any are found, increase diligence in the above efforts.

Seizures, difficulty breathing, or collapse near an electrical cord are signs your dog may have suffered a serious shock while you were away.

For all electric shock accidents, seek immediate veterinary help, even if there is no evidence of injury. Sometimes electric current can bypass the mouth area, leaving no marks, yet cause life-threatening internal damage. In other cases where the injury appears to be mild, more serious damage may not be visible for days after the incident.

For complete first-aid instructions, see page 118.

SAFETY STORY: Sassy's Shocking Mistake

One evening, while I was playing ball with our miniature dachshund, Sassy, the tennis ball rolled under the sofa. About that time, the phone rang. While I was on the phone, Sassy dove under the sofa looking for the ball. Instead of retrieving the ball, she bit down on an extension cord. Suddenly, I heard loud frantic yipping noises coming from Sass. I looked under the sofa and could see Sassy with the cord in her mouth. She was writhing around on the floor with her teeth clenched onto the cord. We quickly threw the breaker switch and pulled Sass out from under the sofa. She cried for a minute or so and then calmed down. We wrapped her in a blanket and took her to the vet. She had minor burns in her mouth but was otherwise fine. The vet said she could have easily died if we hadn't disconnected the power so quickly. Moral of the story: Don't allow your small pets to go under the sofa if you can't see what they're doing, and use covers on your electric cords.

—*Kathy Love, Milwaukie, Oregon*

BURN PREVENTION TIPS

- Keep your dog out of the kitchen while cooking, frying, boiling, or carrying any hot items.

- Keep your dog at a safe distance when grilling or cooking over an open flame. He may be attracted to the smell of meat cooking and wind up in the line of fire, so to speak.

- Use caution while engaging in home or automotive repairs or other projects in which bleach, turpentine, swimming pool cleaners, gasoline, motor oil, or other caustic substances are used. Dogs often like to be near their owners while they work and can be burned by these dangerous chemicals.

Heat and Chemical Burns

Heat and chemical burns don't happen to dogs very often, but they are horribly painful ... and largely preventable. Burns are usually the result of a dog or puppy getting underfoot in the kitchen, nosing around the grill, getting trapped in a house fire, or having caustic chemicals spilled on his fur.

Always seek immediate veterinary assistance for a burn, even if it appears to be mild. Oftentimes a dog's fur can mask deeper damage, and in the case of chemical burns, the fur can trap a chemical and continue burning the dog even if the substance seems to have been removed. (First-aid instructions for burns can be found on page 134.)

MOVE IT, PLEASE!

Dogs that are not taught to move out of the way of a passing human are at risk of being accidentally tripped over, causing serious injuries to the dog, the person, or both. This is especially true with dogs that like to lie in unsafe places like the top of the stairs or right in the middle of the kitchen. Little dogs that get stepped on can suffer broken bones, or dogs in the kitchen can have hot liquids spilled on them. To avoid this type of accident, teach your dog to move whenever he's blocking the path of a person. One way to do this is by bumping into him "accidentally," surprising or jolting him out of the way (don't hurt him, of course; just bump him enough so he gets the idea and moves). Don't look at the dog while you do it—just pretend you're distracted and you didn't see him. Repeat this "bumping into" exercise at regular intervals until he starts moving on his own when he sees he is in the way. It might seem cruel to make your dog get up all the time, especially if he is resting, but it is for your dog's own safety—and everyone else's.

Although your dog may love to "help out" in the kitchen, be sure he can't get underfoot and trip you—especially while you're carrying hot items from the stove or oven.

SAFETY STORY: Isley's Kitchen Catastrophe

It was a gray, overcast summer day. Isley, the puppy I was raising for Canine Companions for Independence (CCI), was napping in front of the kitchen sink after a morning of training and play at the park. I was cooking lunch and had a heat-and-serve pouch of lentils in a pot of boiling water on the stove. As I carried the pot from the stove to the sink, my hands slipped somehow and suddenly, the pot was falling to the ground—right where poor Isley was innocently sleeping. He awoke screaming from the pain of the scalding hot water spilling down his back and right side. I was barely able to contain him as he ran from the kitchen. I rushed him to a nearby emergency animal hospital. As I entered the hospital and explained what happened, they immediately took him to a treatment room. I had held it together very well until that point. But the minute the leash left my hand, I broke down. How could I have hurt this innocent, beloved pup so badly? Was he ruined as a potential service dog?

Isley had second- and third-degree burns on his back and his right side. He spent the night in the hospital, on morphine for the pain. The next day he saw an animal dermatologist. What followed was a month of nightly therapy baths, weekly visits to the dermatologist, acupuncture for pain, and three months later, reconstructive surgery. The reconstructive specialist removed the dead skin, and because Isley was a young dog, she was able to "stretch" his good skin over the burned area.

With the hard work of some amazing veterinarians, Isley pulled through the entire ordeal like a trooper. To see him today, you would never know the accident occurred. There is a very fine scar line and he is a happy, healthy dog. With the love, prayers, and support from my CCI family, I made it through one of the most horrific experiences of my life. The lesson learned will never be forgotten. Anytime I am cooking, the kitchen is off-limits to the dogs. The pups are crated or tethered in another room until they are trained to do a reliable "stay" in the adjoining room. I am happy to say that my fellow CCI puppy raisers, my family, friends, and neighbors have all learned from my experience.

—*Theresa Barnes, CCI puppy raiser, Laguna Niguel, California*

Holiday Hazards

Holidays are a time for celebration, but for dog owners they should also be a time for heightened awareness. The abundance of food, treats, decorations, gifts, and parties in the home bring with them a few additional things to be on the lookout for. By noting the potential hazards in this section and following some of the tips below, you'll be able to relax and enjoy all the celebrations throughout the year without worry.

FOOD ITEMS

Turkey skin, cooked bones like turkey and ham bones, fat trimmings, yeast dough, chocolate, candies and sweets containing xylitol, raisins, alcoholic beverages.

DECORATIONS/LIGHTING

Holiday and decorative ornaments and ornament hooks, small figurines, tinsel, ribbon, tape, streamers, plastic Easter grass and plastic Easter eggs, holiday lights, extension cords.

PLANTS

Mistletoe, holly and holly berries, pine needles, Christmas tree water (which can contain harmful fertilizers, tree preservatives, and bacteria), tulip and amaryllis bulbs.

MISCELLANEOUS

Candles, potpourri, batteries, children's toys, foils, and corks from wine bottles.

Holiday Lights. A variety of lights and electric-powered decorations are holiday staples, and with them come an abundance of electrical and extension cords. To avoid electric shock accidents, keep loose cords bundled and taped up to the wall if possible, unplug cords when not in use, and give them a liberal spritzing of bitter spray if you have a dog or puppy that likes to chew.

Christmas Tree Tactics. Avoid placing the Christmas tree in front of your dog's favorite "lookout window." The tree can be knocked over by an eager dog, sending ornaments crashing to the ground, which can lead to cut paws—not to mention a huge mess. Another

myth busters: 🐕
poinsettias

For years, poinsettias have gotten a bad rap for being highly poisonous and even deadly, but it turns out these colorful holiday plants are not nearly as toxic as once believed. While it's not exactly clear how the rumor began or became so widespread, pet poison control centers now confirm that poinsettias, if ingested by a dog, will cause little more than mild to moderate gastrointestinal upset.

Ribbon and tinsel are potential choking hazards, so these will need to be put away before she wakes up.

way to prevent the tree from being knocked over is to anchor it to a ceiling beam or wall in two places with fishing line.

Hang breakable ornaments toward the top of the tree and save the nonbreakable ones for the lower part. Avoid edible ornaments. Check the floor carefully for any wayward ornament hooks, which can cause serious damage if swallowed.

If your dog seems overly curious about the tree or the gifts under it, or tries to drink the water in the tree stand, use an electronic training mat to keep him away when you're too busy to monitor his behavior.

Ribbons, Decorations, and Wrapping Paper. Wrapping gifts can be fun but messy business, leaving behind scraps of tape, ribbon, and foil. These are all potential choking and obstruction hazards, so be sure to clean up carefully when you're through. Glittery tinsel is attractive to many dogs and puppies and can seriously damage the intestinal tract if swallowed, so you may want to keep it out of the home altogether.

Resist the urge to tie ribbons and bows around your dog's neck. They can get caught on gates and fences, and as just mentioned, are dangerous if swallowed.

Be aware that many snow globes contain toxic antifreeze, so be sure to display them where they can't get knocked over and break open.

Plastic Easter basket grass is a potential choking and intestinal obstruction hazard. If your dog is the type to gobble this up, consider a safer alternative such as straw or shredded color comics section of the newspaper.

Holiday Food, Treats, and Cooking Items. Every holiday comes with guests—and unfortunately, every guest usually comes bearing little boxes of chocolate, foil-wrapped candies, nuts, and fruitcakes. Since these can all be problematic to your dog, be sure to stow them out of reach of your little party animal.

Carefully dispose of the string used to wrap holiday roasts and hams, wooden skewers, cooking foil, plastic wrap, and other items that wind up covered in meat juice. These choking hazards can all be extremely enticing to an otherwise well-behaved dog. Seal them in a plastic bag in the trash, and be sure the trash is securely stored and can't be knocked over. Remove the kitchen trash from the house often during the holidays to avoid problems.

Toys and Batteries. Especially in homes with children, the holidays usually include an increase in batteries and battery-containing toys and games lying about. Be sure these are picked up and that no loose batteries are rolling around under the sofa, since they can be toxic if swallowed.

Noise, Commotion, Costumes, and Fireworks. Be sensitive to your dog's fears and insecurities with strange visitors, noisy parties, fireworks, and costumes, which can be unsettling for canines. Keep your dog in a safe, quiet place if he seems disturbed by these holiday happenings, and be especially mindful with puppies—they can be easily overwhelmed by new experiences and a dozen people all wanting to pet and hold them at once.

At the same time, be sensitive to your guests, too! Your dog may love to party, but not everyone loves a dog that jumps up, barks, or begs. Children and elderly guests can be injured if knocked over by an exuberant dog.

Trick or treat? If you opt for the treat, remember that chocolate is a no-no for dogs—but carob-coated dog treats are a safe and delicious alternative.

safety tip:
holiday gifts for dogs

With each impending holiday, many pet shops gear up with a variety of holiday-themed toys and gift bags. These may seem like the perfect present for your furry friend, but use caution when making a selection: Since these toys are seasonal and have a short life on the store shelf, they are often cheaply constructed and can be ripped apart easily, presenting a choking or obstruction hazard. This doesn't mean your pooch can't celebrate, of course—just choose wisely and supervise play until you're certain the new toy is able to withstand your dog's chewing habits.

four

THE GARAGE, BACKYARD, AND BEYOND: KEEPING SAFE IN THE GREAT OUTDOORS

Dogs love venturing outdoors, and for good reason—there's no better place to stretch those legs, smell the roses (and other less-than-rosy smelling things), and enjoy a satisfying romp with their favorite people and playmates. A dog's curiosity is heightened by the ever-changing sights and smells outside—even in their own backyard, where harmful garden products, chemicals, toxic plants, and other hazards are sometimes found. This chapter will show you how to create a safe backyard haven for your dog or puppy, deal with seasonal safety issues, and avoid some common accidents that happen during canine travel and adventure.

Backyard Safety: Plants, Poisons, Pools, and More

All backyards are different; each has its own unique requirements for becoming a dog-safe retreat. Even a very small space with no greenery must be properly fenced, have no raised decks or balconies a dog or puppy could fall from, and offer adequate protection from the elements. Other outdoor spaces are so vast they're nearly impossible to securely fence and police for hazards. In these cases, consider fencing off a more manageable portion. Once you've defined the space your dog will have access to, you'll need to make it comfortable and free from dangerous plants, pests, and chemicals, as well as physical and weather-related hazards.

FENCING

The primary goal of fencing is to safely contain the dog on your property to prevent her from escaping, becoming lost, being hit by a car, or getting otherwise injured. Wood, iron, chain link, vinyl—it doesn't matter what the fence is made of, as long as it prevents the dog from squeezing through, digging under, jumping over, or being injured by gaps or sharp edges.

Holes and Gaps. Repairing holes and gaps in your fence prevents your dog from leaving and keeps other dogs and critters from entering your yard. It also minimizes the likelihood of strangers teasing or poking sticks through to torment the dog. A dog can get her head or body caught in gaps or slats that are too wide. Attaching chicken wire along the bottom half of an otherwise-sturdy fence can often solve this problem.

Sharp Edges. If your dog engages in "running the fence," lunging at passing dogs, or just hanging out close to the fence, make sure there are no sharp edges that can cut her, or worse, snag the collar and potentially cause a strangulation. The edges of chain link are often a culprit here—especially along the bottom, where a dog can get her paws caught if the fence isn't buried below ground level.

Digging to Freedom. Determined diggers can tunnel their way out of seemingly impenetrable fences with alarming success. If you have an expert digger on your hands, try the following tactics:

- Lay a one-foot (30 cm)-wide length of chain link or chicken wire on the ground along the fence, and anchor it in place. Dogs hate the sensation of having their toenails caught in the wire, so this creates a strong deterrent to digging. You can also bury chicken wire a couple of inches underground along the fence line for the same effect.

- Place cinder blocks or large rocks along the base of the fence, pounded deeply into the soil to hold them in place.

- Bury the bottom of the fence one to two feet (30 to 60 cm) below ground level.

The Right Height. Dogs that grow up with fences from an early age tend to respect the visual barrier no matter what the height. For most dogs, an average fence height of four feet (1.2 m) is enough to keep them on the right side. If you have a "jumper," however, you'll need to increase the height of your fence to a minimum of six feet (1.8 m). For extreme cases, some have attached a short "prison fence" along the top of the fence—chain link that is angled back toward the yard. It may not be attractive, but it works to keep even the most talented jumpers from escaping.

safety tip:
gate safety

A great way to keep your dog safely confined to your property is to install double gates in your backyard (like the kind you see at dog parks). This added security measure can prevent the gate from being accidentally left open by children, gardeners, and other people who come and go throughout the day. If putting in a double gate isn't feasible, install springs on the hinges so the gate snaps closed automatically.

Electronic Fences. Electronic pet containment fencing, also known as invisible fencing, is a viable containment option for many situations, but it has definite upsides and downsides. The system consists of a thin wire that runs along the desired boundary perimeter (up to 20 acres [8 ha] or so), a transmitter, and a collar that the dog wears. Little flags or another visual aid are usually placed at regular intervals along the wire to provide the dog with a visual cue of the boundary. As the dog approaches the boundary, she hears an audible warning tone. If she gets too close or crosses the boundary, the collar gives her a safe but effective shock to keep her contained.

The upside to an electronic fence is that if you have a large property, it's much more affordable than installing a physical fence. It maintains the beauty of large open spaces by not obstructing the view. It can even be used around swimming pools and flowerbeds to protect both your canine and your camellias.

The downsides are that while electronic fences may effectively keep your dog in, they do nothing to keep other animals—or intruders—out. Another pitfall is that some dogs who like to chase after birds, rodents, bicyclers, etc., can get so pumped full of adrenaline during the chase that they run right through the boundary without even feeling the shock. When they've calmed down and decide to return home, the shock component actually works in reverse, preventing them from wanting to cross back through to their home turf. Electronic fences are also not recommended for areas exposed to road traffic.

TOXIC PLANTS AND OTHER GARDEN HAZARDS

More than 100 plants are known to be toxic to pets. Fortunately, not all of them are likely to be in your garden, most of them taste pretty bad, and most won't cause serious problems unless significant quantities are ingested. That said, some common backyard plants are so highly toxic they can harm a dog even in small quantities, such as **sago palm**, **oleander**, and **castor bean**. What's more, there are no legal requirements to disclose this information at the point of purchase, so little information is offered that would prevent pet owners from purchasing such plants at their local garden center and placing them in their yard. To be on the safe side, it's important to know what you have in your yard and remove or replace the bad stuff with dog-friendly alternatives.

Using dog-friendly garden plants and products allows you to spend more time together without worrying what your pooch may get into.

identifying toxic plants

In the appendixes, you'll find a complete Toxic Plant Guide (pages 149–155) to help you analyze the plants in your home and garden. Ask your gardener or landscaper for assistance or bring clippings to a local nursery for identification. Many nurseries or garden centers will also send someone to your home for a reasonable fee.

In addition to plants, many flower bulbs are also toxic to pets. These include amaryllis, daffodil (narcissus), and hyacinth. Be sure all bulbs are stored securely out of reach of your dog and keep an eye out for any digging once planted.

10 COMMON TOXIC BACKYARD PLANTS

Azalea
(*Rhododendron* spp.)

Kalanchoe
(*Kalanchoe* spp.)

Castor Bean
(*Ricinus communis*)

Oleander
(*Nerium oleander*)

Cyclamen
(*Cyclamen* spp.)

Pothos
(*Scindapsus* spp.)

Dumb Cane
(*Dieffenbachia 'exotica'*)

Sago Palm
(*Cycas* spp.)

Foxglove
(*Digitalis purpurea*)

Yew
(*Taxus cuspidata*)

SAFETY STORY: Puppy Puppy and the Sago Palm

My three-year-old Cavalier King Charles spaniel, Puppy Puppy, was my constant companion. She rode with me in the car, went on all our family trips, and slept snuggled up to my cheek every night. She especially loved our daily long walks through the neighborhood. I considered myself an extremely responsible pet owner. I used quality pet food, had a fenced-in yard, safe toys, nontoxic cleaning products, and scheduled regular vet appointments.

One night, I noticed Puppy Puppy was not following at my heels as usual. I found her huddled in the corner of a closet, throwing up. I assumed it was just something she ate—although she was no longer a puppy by age, she still chewed on things. I stayed with her until she seemed okay and carried her to bed. In the middle of the night, I heard her vomiting again. This time, she had glazed eyes and was totally lethargic. At this point I knew something was very wrong and took her to the vet. Later, the vet called to say she was in serious condition, and they'd be keeping her overnight. She seemed to have ingested poison. We searched the house for anything she could have gotten into, even asking the neighbors about any poisons they may have used in the yard. In searching her dog bed, I found a half-eaten seed that looked unusual. When I told the vet, she asked if we had Sago palms. We didn't think so but searched our property. To our horror, we found an old Sago palm in the far corner of our yard, left by the previous owner. It was not a healthy plant but was still producing seeds. Sure enough, the Sago palm seed matched what I found in her dog bed. This was not good news. Sago palm is deadly to dogs—if ingested, it destroys the liver. Puppy was receiving treatment, but the doctors had little hope. She survived nine days in ICU. Since Puppy's death, I've worked hard to spread the word of this danger. I can only hope my story helps pet owners understand the serious danger of the Sago palm and remove them from their property.

—*Bridget Styles, Houston, Texas*

DOGGIE DAMAGE CONTROL:
DIGGING

It's natural for dogs to dig, especially breeds like dachshunds and smaller terriers that were bred to hunt rodents. In addition to tunneling for "critters," dogs also dig to bury bones or toys, to make a hole to lie in when they're hot, or just for the fun of it. Dogs left alone in the yard might dig out of frustration. Whatever the reason, you'd no doubt like to curtail this behavior right away.

The best solution, and one that doesn't squelch your dog's natural instincts, is to create an approved "digging pit" somewhere in your yard and have this be the *only* place you allow the dog to dig. Build a sandbox and fill it with sand or dirt (sand is easier to clean off paws). Encourage your dog by placing a few toys just under the surface and leading her to the area. When she digs there, tell her "Good dig!" If she tries to dig anywhere outside of her sandbox, stop her with a firm "No!" and lead her over to the sandbox. Wait for her to dig in the sand again and repeat the praise. To help make the training successful in the first week or two, don't let her in the yard unless you can supervise her and enforce the proper digging location. Soon enough, she should get the hang of the new rules.

However, some dogs find a spot in the garden that's so appealing, they refuse to stop digging there. To discourage this, place chicken wire just below the top layer of soil. After a few tries she'll most likely give up and view the sandbox with more enthusiasm.

Pesticides, Insecticides, and Rodenticides

Most garden products designed for residential use are generally safe, provided you follow the directions and wait the recommended length of time before allowing your dog back in the treated area. That said, some garden products are so nasty they account for numerous fatal poisonings each year. The worst of these are snail baits containing metaldehyde. Using these poison pellets, which are formulated with molasses and bran to attract their victims, is akin to throwing kibble all over the yard. Dogs love the smell and taste, and ingesting even a small quantity can be deadly. The bottom line is to avoid this type of snail bait at all costs if you have dogs. Instead, choose one of the effective, pet-safe alternatives containing iron phosphate, which are widely available in nurseries and garden centers (see Resources, page 157).

Systemic insecticides containing disulfoton (typically found in rose and flower foods) are also highly toxic and should be avoided. Poisonings usually occur when dog owners mix the disulfoton product with blood or bone meal to fertilize roses—the blood and bone meal attracts the dog. The word *systemic* on a label should make you suspicious. Occasionally, potted roses are treated with disulfoton, so always inquire about this at the nursery.

Other garden no-nos are fly baits containing methomyl and underground rodent poisons, both of which typically come in granular form and have a sweet taste that attracts dogs. Despite the fact that rodent baits are buried and fly baits can be hung high in a trap, it's simply not worth the risk.

Snail and slug baits containing metaldehyde are one of the most common causes of fatal poisoning in dogs.

Fortunately, today there are more natural, environmentally safe, and pet-friendly garden products than ever before. As long as you read labels carefully, follow directions, and ask nursery employees for assistance if you have questions, you and your dog should be able to enjoy the backyard and garden without worry.

DOGGIE DAMAGE CONTROL:
URINE SPOTS ON GRASS

If you have a dog and a lawn, you probably have a few telltale brown patches on the grass to show for it. You can greatly reduce these dreaded urine spots with a little diligence, simply by hosing them down thoroughly as soon after they happen as possible. Even if you do this a day or two later it can reduce the damage. How? Urine contains a high concentration of nitrogen, which is responsible for burning the grass. Therefore, hosing it down dilutes the nitrogen and reduces the burn spots.

To repair the spots that are already there, you'll have to dig them up, thoroughly soak the ground beneath them, and reseed the lawn. Then keep up the practice of hosing down the urine once the grass grows in.

Think twice about buying one of the many dietary supplements out there designed to "eliminate" lawn burn. They may be safe for your dog, but that doesn't make them healthy. If you'd like to try altering your dog's diet to help reduce the problem, speak with your vet about finding a more highly digestible or lower-protein food, which may cut back on the amount of nitrogen expelled in the urine.

Yard and Garden Safety Odds and Ends

- Check your garden regularly and remove any toadstools or wild mushrooms you find—some varieties can be very toxic if ingested.
- Block off compost piles, which may contain hazardous molds and toxins.
- Set pop-up sprinklers so that they sit as flush to ground level as possible when not in their "pop-up" mode, and survey your yard for other physical hazards like rakes, metal stakes, or decorative garden art the dog might injure herself on while running or playing.
- When purchasing garden mulch, check the label to make sure it's not "cocoa bean mulch." As the name implies, this type of mulch is actually made from cocoa and contains the same toxic principle as chocolate. Its unique smell and taste inspires many dogs to eat it, and if enough is consumed it can cause severe diarrhea, vomiting, neurological effects, and in rare cases, can be fatal.

Outdoor Pests and Other Animal Hazards

Just about every region has its share of native pests and wild critters that can make life difficult for local dogs. Naturally they can't all be covered here, but in many cases the risk of exposure can be reduced by commonsense tactics. These include not keeping dog food and water dishes outdoors (assuming the dog always has access to fresh water inside), securely storing outdoor trash, keeping dogs leashed on nature walks, and in some cases, training them to avoid the problem altogether, such as with snake avoidance training.

Bees, Wasps, and Spiders. Dogs rarely get stung by bees or wasps unless they try to play with or nip at them. When they do, the resulting sting is usually somewhere on the face or in the mouth, causing minor itching, swelling, and redness that can be treated with simple first aid such as a cold compress and baking soda poultice. This is also the case with most spider bites, although you should always attempt to identify the spider and call a vet to ensure it's not venomous or life threatening. Examples of venomous spiders are widows (known for the red hourglass shape on their undersides) and the brown recluse (identified by the dark, violin-shaped marking on the top of its body).

Some dogs may have *severe allergic reactions* to bites and stings. Their faces swell tremendously, and the dog may paw at the face and act distressed. Although not common, there's also a possibility that the swelling can affect a dog's ability to breathe. To ensure an allergic reaction doesn't turn dangerous, always take your dog to the vet if facial swelling develops. An injection of antihistamine and/or steroid may be necessary.

The most severe type of reaction to an insect sting is *anaphylactic shock*. Although rare, you will know immediately when it happens because the dog will experience vomiting, diarrhea, difficulty breathing, and can collapse and die within minutes. Be prepared to perform CPR (see page 122) and rush to the nearest emergency hospital. (See Insect Stings and Snake Bites on page 142 for first-aid instructions.)

Bufo Toads. Certain species of Bufo toad (*Bufo marinus* and *Bufo alvarius*) secrete a toxic mucus that can be very hazardous to dogs that come into contact with them. Found throughout North America (especially in tropical locations like Florida and Hawaii, as well as parts of the Southwest), these toads are most active in the summer months and can sometimes be found sitting in dogs' water dishes. Exposed dogs will drool, shake their head, paw at the mouth, and vomit. Severe cases can be fatal without prompt veterinary treatment. If you think your dog has been exposed to Bufo toad poisoning, rinse her mouth thoroughly with a slow, steady stream from a garden hose and seek immediate veterinary treatment.

Fire Ants. Dogs are usually exposed to fire ants while running or digging near an ant mound. They can also be stung while lying on the ground near an ant trail, or when the ants swarm a dog's outdoor food dish. One or two stings from a fire ant usually results in mild pain, redness, and itching, which you would treat similar to a bee sting. Dogs that suffer multiple stings from a disturbed mound can have severe reactions, especially dogs that are very old, young, in poor health, or have open sores such as hot spots.

The ants usually sting a dog's underside, ears, face, and other areas where there's minimal hair. If multiple fire ants attack your dog, quickly remove her from the source and wipe the ants away thoroughly with a damp towel (do not rinse the dog with a hose, as this usually has little effect). Call your vet for treatment advice, watch the dog closely, and be prepared to take her to the vet if she appears to be developing a severe reaction.

If you discover active fire ant mounds on your property, try pouring a few gallons (11L) of boiling water over the mound to kill them. If the problem is widespread, consult a pest control professional for advice on how to safely exterminate them.

Snakes. If there are poisonous snakes in your region, you most likely have concerns about your dog when you venture outdoors together—especially if your dog is prone to investigating wild animals. One method of prevention that's grown in popularity is *snake avoidance training*. This process involves a skilled dog trainer, a remote training collar for your dog, and up to several poisonous snakes indigenous to your region, which are humanely muzzled. A controlled environment is set up in which the dog will "encounter" the snake either by sight, smell, or sound (in the case of rattlesnakes).

The moment the dog encounters the snake, the remote collar emits a safe, low-level shock to the dog, teaching them that—ouch!—snakes are bad. When considering snake avoidance training for your dog, it's important to ensure the trainer is reputable, skilled, and that all the animals are treated humanely. Your veterinarian or local humane society is usually a good resource for finding the right trainer.

A relatively new rattlesnake vaccine is also available for dogs—it does not offer full protection from a bite, but buys you a little more time to get emergency treatment. Consider this vaccine only if a dog is frequently in the field (for example, hunting dogs) or

is resistant to snake training, as many in the veterinary community are concerned about the long-term health effects of unnecessary vaccines. Your veterinarian can help you decide if the vaccine is right for your dog.

See page 143 for a guide to common poisonous snakes.

Porcupines. Porcupines are generally shy creatures that want nothing to do with a dog. Unfortunately, not all dogs comply with this wish and wind up with a face full of quills. If just a few quills are present and there are none in the mouth or eyes, you can pull them out yourself if the dog will let you. Approach the dog calmly, have someone help you to restrain her, grasp the quill firmly near the base with pliers, and pull it out. Wash the area to prevent infection. If there are many quills or they're located in the mouth or another delicate area, have them safely removed by a vet, who may also prescribe an antibiotic.

THE GARAGE AND OUTDOOR SHEDS

Garages and storage sheds are typically the place one keeps all the stuff they wouldn't want anywhere near their living space—chemicals, paint, automotive supplies, sharp tools, and sporting goods. It's also a place where nails, screws, rodent traps, and leaks from under a car are less likely to be cleaned off the floor in a timely manner. A dog can get into trouble pretty quickly in such a place if precautions are not taken. For example, **antifreeze made with ethylene glycol is so toxic that just a few tablespoons (45 ml) can kill a dog.** It has a sweet taste and can leak from under a car unnoticed, until the owner drives away and the dog wanders in and licks it up. Thankfully, there are now more pet-safe antifreezes available that contain propylene glycol as the active ingredient.

If your dog can access the garage, take care to ensure that these types of hazards are out of her reach. Keep storage and garden sheds locked. And remember, when dog proofing these areas, don't just think poisons … think choking hazards, sharp objects, large bags of kibble, and so on.

protecting wildlife *and* your dog

If your dog has a history of disturbing porcupines or other small animals, keep her leashed on hikes and in wooded areas, and don't let her investigate woodpiles, brush, ponds, or other places where troublesome critters may congregate.

Garage Hazards

Antifreeze, motor oil, and other automotive fluids

Barbecue briquettes and lighter fluid

Cocoa bean shell mulch (cocoa mulch)

Fertilizers, plant food, and flower bulbs

Fish hooks, fishing weights, and other tackle

Golf balls and racquetballs

Ice-melting products and road salt

Insecticides and pesticides

Lead shot

Nails, nuts, and bolts

Paint, paint thinners, and turpentine

Paintball pellets

Plant food and fertilizers

Rodent traps and baits

Sharp tools

Swimming pool treatment supplies

When purchasing antifreeze, always choose a less toxic, "pet-safe" formulation containing propylene glycol.

PROTECTION FROM THE ELEMENTS

For dogs that spend time in the backyard (and cannot come and go as they please via a dog door), providing adequate protection from the elements is essential. In cold weather, she'll need a warm, dry place to sleep that's shielded from wind, rain, and snow. On warm days she'll need continuous shade. If the weather is hot or the dog is a candidate for heatstroke (see Heatstroke [Hyperthermia], page 140), a child's plastic wading pool filled with water will help keep her cool and happy. Naturally, a large, sturdy water dish with plenty of fresh water is a must in any climate. For comfort and security, a well-designed doghouse is a good choice.

Despite those pleading expressions, it's best to keep dogs inside and out of the way while working with power tools or harsh chemicals like turpentine.

DOGHOUSE HOW-TOS

Design. If you live in a cold or wet climate, choose a doghouse with a tightly sealed, slanted roof and raised floor to provide insulation from the cold and damp. An off-center entrance helps shield the dog from heavy winds by letting her curl up in the far corner.

Size. Unless you have a puppy and are buying a size up for the future, choose one that is just large enough to allow your dog to stand upright, turn around easily, and lie down comfortably. The goal is to create a cozy den. For a puppy, stuff blankets in the extra space until she grows into it.

Location. Placing the doghouse near the backyard entrance to your home allows her to monitor the comings and going of the people inside, without feeling isolated. Be sure the spot has good drainage for wet weather. If you live in a warm climate, placing it in the shade will help keep the internal temperature cool.

Bedding. A soft material should be put down on the floor to make a nice bed. This could be a kennel pad, blankets, or even straw. Whatever you choose, be sure it's easy to clean or, if using hay or straw, can be changed regularly.

Introducing Your Dog to Her Doghouse

Schedule some time when the weather isn't extreme and you can set a chair near the doghouse and hang out with her for an hour or so with a good book. You might place an old shirt or something with your scent on it inside the house, along with a favorite toy. Then, crouch down near the entrance and call her over, placing a nice treat inside. Don't force it if she's wary. Just relax and continue sitting nearby until her curiosity gets the better of her, or crawl in yourself and act very impressed. You can also try feeding her regularly inside her house to create a positive association, or if she fetches, throwing her ball inside in the middle of a game.

Lastly, keep in mind that while a backyard/doghouse-only setup might be great for a few hours of the day, most dogs really want to be inside where their human family resides, even when you're not there.

POOL SAFETY

Most dogs fall into two categories: those that love to swim and those that avoid the water at all costs. Even if your pooch is an enthusiastic swimmer, that doesn't mean she should have an all-access pool pass. Any dog can drown in a backyard pool, so rule number one is never let your dog swim or hang around the pool without supervision!

Never let your dog swim or hang around the pool without supervision!

A self-closing fence around your pool is essential, particularly in homes with puppies, nonswimmers, and elderly dogs. If you have young children, you likely have a fence already. If not, there are a variety of options to fit a range of budgets and tastes. Some may think fences spoil the backyard aesthetic, but having one offers invaluable peace of mind.

The next priority for pool safety is to **have a clearly marked, easy-to-use exit**. Place a potted plant or flag near the steps and leave it there permanently, so the dog can easily find the exit if she becomes disoriented. Make sure the water covering the top step is shallow enough to allow your dog to comfortably enter and exit the pool. If not, you'll need a pool ramp.

Another safety measure is **to install a pool alarm** that alerts you whenever the surface of the water is broken. There are many types of pool alarms, some made especially for dogs where a device on the collar alerts you if the dog falls in. This type of alarm is essential if you have a backyard pond that's impossible to fence.

Avoid using soft pool covers. A dog can easily mistake one for a solid surface and step onto it, or fall in and become trapped underneath it.

Teaching a Dog to Swim

Before you teach a nonswimmer to swim, keep in mind that some dogs may be ill-suited for this activity. These include young puppies; elderly or overweight dogs; short-nosed, short-legged, or toy breeds; and dogs with medical conditions. Other dogs simply don't like the water, and that's okay—never force a fearful dog to swim. Dogs without tails may have trouble when learning to swim, since the tail is used as a rudder—but they'll soon find their own technique to make it work if they like the water.

Know in advance that you will be going into the pool with your dog, and have another person there to help you. If possible, make that person a friend with a water-loving dog, who may actually teach your dog to swim before you ever get your feet wet!

1. Sit on the top step and lure your dog over to you with her favorite toy or treat (cut-up hot dogs work wonders here). Use a leash to guide her onto the step if necessary.

2. Once she's comfortable there, wrap both arms gently under her belly and slowly guide her into the water.

3. Bring her just a few feet (about a meter) from the steps, position her facing directly toward them, and let her paddle toward the steps, keeping your arms in position for guidance.

4. Have your helper waiting at the top of the steps to grab her collar if needed to guide her out. Then, heap on the praise, wait a few moments, and repeat the process, this time taking her further from the steps.

5. Keep the lesson short unless the dog seems interested in continuing. Otherwise, schedule another lesson within the next few days, and repeat until she has the hang of it, gradually increasing the distance each time. Make it fun by using fetching toys, treats, and lots of praise.

safety tip:
drinking pool or pond water

Don't let your dog get into the habit of drinking pool water, and never let her drink from spas or garden ponds. In addition to chlorine and other bad chemicals, drinking algae (particularly blue-green algae in ponds) can be very dangerous. To discourage this, keep a water dish nearby.

Preventing Collar Accidents

There's no disputing that collars and leashes are vital, essential equipment for dogs and their owners. What some people don't know is that these very items that help keep dogs safe can also be deadly in certain situations. Collar accidents are the most frequent cause of strangulation in dogs, and they often take place at home, in the backyard, even under supervision—and can happen with many types of collars. Typically, a dog's collar or ID tags get caught on a fence, branch, gate, heating vent, or on the wire of a kennel or crate, and in the ensuing panic and struggle to free herself, the dog strangles.

Another scenario is when two or more dogs are playing and one dog's jaw gets caught on the other's collar. This tends to happen at dog parks when dogs are left to run and wrestle while wearing chain or prong collars. Even with immediate human intervention, the tension is often too tight to remove the collar or separate the dogs in time.

Sometimes collar accidents are caused by the unsafe use of leashes or tie-outs. Imagine that a dog is tied up on a raised deck, balcony, or in the back of an open vehicle and either falls accidentally or decides to run after a squirrel or another dog. If the leash or tie-out isn't long enough to reach the ground or gets caught on something, the dog literally hangs herself. If a dog is tethered to a pole and circles it enough times to get tangled, she can strangle herself in the struggle to break free.

Whenever possible, remove collars while dogs play to avoid a wayward jaw getting caught during a rambunctious wrestling match.

Protect your dog from collar and leash accidents by following these tips:

- Remove collars whenever possible while dogs play together (*do not do this in any area that's not safely enclosed and free from road traffic*).

- Use a quick-release snap buckle collar or a "break-away" collar designed to snap free if snagged or caught on an object. Avoid traditional belt buckle–style collars, which are difficult to remove quickly in an emergency.

- Avoid chain collars or prong collars. If you must use one to walk your dog, remove it whenever she is off leash.

- Avoid dangling ID tags whenever possible. Look for collars that let you handwrite or engrave your contact information directly on the collar, or one with a riveted nameplate that attaches to the collar's flat surface. If there are tags the dog must wear, attaching them to a breakaway collar offers protection against dangerous snags.

- Never tie your dog up on a raised surface or in the back of an open vehicle. If you must tie her up somewhere on ground level, be sure it is free of obstacles and cannot be "circled around" to avoid entanglement.

- Check your dog's collar regularly to ensure proper fit: You should be able to just slip two or three fingers between the collar and your dog's neck. If a collar is too loose, the dog's jaw or leg can become stuck in it. If it is too tight it can restrict breathing or cause damage to the trachea, especially in puppies and toy breeds.

SAFETY STORY: Jack's Tragedy

I had two dogs named Einstein and Jack that loved to play together. One day after church, the dogs were outside with my husband and son, and Einstein's lower jaw got caught in Jack's collar while they were playing. Both dogs panicked and tried to get free, but it only caused the collar to twist and tighten. My husband and son were there in an instant, but they could not get the collar free. I ran to get a knife, but the collar was pulled so tight we couldn't cut it off. My husband was finally able to break the plastic latch and get the collar off, but it was too late for Jack. He had died from strangulation. It was the most tragic day of my life, and the memories of not being able to save him haunt us all. I have since learned about breakaway collars and am spreading the word so that no one else has to go through what we did.

—*Barb Oneal, Corunna, Indiana*

If your dog is strangling:

1. Cut the collar off immediately with heavy scissors, a bolt cutter, or garden shears. Cut it off from the back of the neck to avoid accidentally cutting major veins.

2. Perform rescue breathing/CPR if necessary (see page 122) and get immediate medical attention if the dog has stopped breathing, even if you quickly revive her.

BREAKAWAY COLLARS

Breakaway collars are designed to prevent collar strangulation by using a safety buckle that releases and literally "breaks away" in emergency situations, such as when a dog becomes entangled on a fence, shrub, or another dog's jaw during play. The breaking strength of the collar depends on the angle of tension and size of the dog, but they are generally engineered to break away with moderate tension. The collars are designed with double rings that, when hooked onto a leash, allow you to walk your dog normally, without the risk of the collar releasing. Should the collar release during an entanglement emergency, it can be reattached afterward and used over and over again. For those concerned that the collar's ability to break away would leave their dog with no identification, many agree that especially if a dog is microchipped, the benefits of the collar far outweigh the risks.

THE DANGER OF RETRACTABLE LEASHES

Retractable leashes are a popular item among many dog owners. Its design allows the leash to extend up to 16 feet (5 m), giving the dog more freedom to sniff, wander, and trot ahead of his owner while walking, which in turn gives the dog owner more freedom to enjoy the walk without having their dog yank them around as they would on a normal length leash. Sounds perfect, right? Wrong! The retractable leash is a danger to dogs, their owners, passers-by, children, other dogs, and just about anyone who goes near one while in use. How dangerous are they? One top-selling leash even features a warning against eye or face injury; cuts, burns, and amputations; and suggests extreme caution when using around infants and children. This disclaimer is followed by two pages of instructions on how not to maim or blind yourself while using the leash. Unless you have an extremely well-behaved dog and are walking alone with no other people or dogs nearby, avoid using this type of leash—and be cautious around others near you who are using one.

If you or your dog should ever become tangled in someone else's retractable leash, immediately yell, "Drop the leash!" It might seem like common sense, but people do not always think rationally when things get hectic.

A child's plastic wading pool is a refreshing, inexpensive way to cool your pooch on a hot summer day. Change the water every day to prevent algae growth.

Hot and Cold Weather Hazards and Other Seasonal Safety Tips

Keeping a dog safe in extremely hot or cold weather requires extra awareness and diligence, no matter what type of dog you have. Naturally, a Saint Bernard will fare better in the snow than a Chihuahua, but that doesn't mean you can't take your Chihuahua along on your next alpine adventure. By learning how to prevent some common weather-related safety hazards, you can enjoy all the seasons with your canine companion.

HEATSTROKE

Dogs don't sweat like we do. Their bodies are designed to conserve heat and contain only a limited number of sweat glands, mainly in the pads of the feet. Their primary means of cooling themselves is through panting, so if the mercury rises and they have only hot air to breathe, they are at great risk of heatstroke. The dog's body temperature rises to dangerous levels, brain and organ damage begins, and the dog can die quickly without immediate emergency treatment. Although heatstroke can happen to any dog, certain types are more at risk: short-nosed breeds like boxers, bulldogs, and pugs (who don't breathe as efficiently as other breeds); dogs that are overweight or in poor physical condition; dogs with heart or lung conditions; and elderly dogs.

Heatstroke most commonly results when a dog is left in a hot car. Even in outside temperatures as low as 72°F (22°C), a car's interior can quickly heat to dangerous levels (see page 104 for more on dogs left in cars). Other causes are overexertion in hot weather (such as when jogging on a hot day with an owner) or simply being outdoors on a hot, humid day with no shade or water.

If a dog shows signs of heat-stroke, your first priority is to safely cool him and seek immediate emergency treatment. See Hyperthermia, page 140, for first-aid instructions.

Signs of Heatstroke

- Bright red gum color in early stages; pale, blue, or gray in late stages
- Panting heavily; thick saliva
- Body temperature above 104°F (40°C)
- Increased heart rate and respiratory rate
- Disorientation, "drunken" behavior, depression
- Vomiting or diarrhea, with or without the presence of blood
- Capillary refill time is too fast (see Capillary Refill Time, page 15)
- Shock (see Shock, page 147)
- Collapse, coma

To prevent heatstroke, keep your dog indoors on hot days if she's in one of the high-risk categories mentioned previously. For other dogs, restrict physical activity to early mornings and evenings, when it's cooler outside; provide plenty of fresh water and shade; and when indoors, set up an electric fan if you do not have air conditioning. **Never leave your dog in a parked car—even with the windows rolled down!** Think twice before taking her with you to outdoor parties, fairs, and other summertime events—you have no way of predicting how crowded it will be or whether there'll be adequate shade and water. If you're looking for something fun to do together, a dip in the pool will provide welcome relief to parched pooches.

safety tip:
easy does it

A dog's paw pads can become very resilient with gradual exposure to outdoor activity. But dogs that don't get out much can experience painful cuts and tears if they suddenly "go for it" without proper conditioning, such as when dogs that are normally couch potatoes let loose at a cage-free boarding facility. Although tears in the paw pad are generally a minor injury that will heal with basic first aid, they can often be avoided by making sure your dog gets regular exercise to gradually toughen up her pads.

Other Warm Weather Hazards

When the air temperature cranks up on a hot day, so do many outdoor surfaces such as asphalt, concrete, brick, and stone pavements. Check the hardscaping in your yard by feeling it in full midday sun. If any areas are too hot, be sure your dog has options and is not forced to lie or walk anywhere she doesn't want to. While out walking on a hot day, avoid hot surfaces like blacktop parking lots. When in doubt, simply feel the ground with your hand—if it feels too hot to you, it probably is. If you notice the dog suddenly picks up her pace after crossing onto a new ground surface, that's a good hint, too.

Many dogs with light skin, pink noses, and thin hair coats are susceptible to sunburn. A pet-safe sunscreen can offer protection. These can be found in pet supply stores and many veterinary clinics.

Warm weather also brings with it an increase in fleas, ticks, and mosquitoes. Keep up with your normal, vet-approved flea and tick preventives, groom your dog often, and never use human mosquito repellents on dogs—even products approved for children can harm them, especially anything containing DEET or pure citronella oil. Ask your vet or pet supply to recommend a dog-safe mosquito repellent if necessary.

In the spring and summer months, foxtails become a hazard to your dog or puppy. Foxtails are the dried seed heads of certain grasses, which can break off and stick to your socks, your shoes, and unfortunately, your dog. If not promptly removed, foxtails can work their way inside a dog's ears, up the nostrils, under the eyelids, and between the toes, so it's important to thoroughly check your dog after each outing and remove any you find. Rest assured, however, that contrary to urban legend, foxtails CANNOT migrate into the brain and kill your dog! A bony plate located in the brain called the cribriform plate would prevent a foxtail from entering the brain region. Signs you may have missed a wayward foxtail elsewhere in the body are intense sneezing (foxtail up the nostril), head shaking (foxtail deep in the ear), and squinting or eye swelling (foxtail under the eyelid). If your dog exhibits any of these signs, the foxtail will have to be removed by a veterinarian. To help prevent your dog from picking up foxtails, carefully trim any long hair around the ears and between the toes.

If your dog stays outdoors in warm weather, ensure backyard hardscaping surfaces are not too hot for her to stand or lie on.

HYPOTHERMIA AND FROSTBITE

Dogs are naturally equipped to tolerate cold temperatures to an impressive degree, especially dense or double-coated breeds like Siberian huskies and Saint Bernards. But there are instances in which prolonged exposure to cold causes a dog's body temperature to drop dangerously low, resulting in hypothermia. This happens most frequently when dogs are small, very young or old, in poor health, thin coated, or when they get wet.

The first sign of hypothermia is shivering, which increases a dog's metabolism and helps her retain heat. This won't work for long though, so it's your cue to get the dog indoors immediately, dry her off if necessary (a hair dryer will help warm her at the same time—just take care to keep it at a safe distance to avoid burns), and wrap her in warm blankets until she stops shivering. Give her warm broth to drink, and if possible, wrap a hot water bottle in a towel and place it next to (but not directly on) her. Take her temperature (see page 15 for instructions) and call your veterinarian for further treatment advice.

Dogs with hypothermia are also at risk for frostbite. When a dog's body temperature drops, blood is naturally diverted to her "core" body to protect the internal organs. This leaves her extremities such as the tips of the ears, the tail, and feet susceptible to freezing. The affected areas of skin will be pale and hard to the touch, the ears may droop slightly, and the dog will limp. Bring the dog indoors immediately and warm the affected areas with warm (not hot) compresses. Do not rub or massage the skin, as this can cause further tissue damage. Call the vet immediately for further treatment advice.

Shivering is the first sign of hypo-thermia. If this happens, bring your dog indoors, dry him off and begin safely warming him.

Luckily, both hypothermia and frostbite are easily preventable. Simply avoid prolonged exposure to frigid temps, adjusting to your dog's individual tolerance level. For smaller, thin-coated dogs, puppies, and other types ill-suited to cold climates, dress them in sweaters, booties, and other cold weather gear. Bring your dog inside and dry her off if she gets wet. And if you have a hardier breed that will be left outdoors for a few hours, make sure she has access to a warm, dry shelter such as a doghouse.

OTHER COLD WEATHER HAZARDS

Dogs that live in snowy climates are often exposed to road salt and other ice-melting products, antifreeze leaks, and other hazardous items that are used to combat freezing temperatures. At home, you can protect your dog by using pet-safe antifreeze and ice-melting products (see Resources, page 157, for suggestions). But since you can't control what other people use, always be sure to wipe your dog down carefully (concentrating on the feet, legs, and stomach) after returning from outdoor activities. This will prevent the dog from possibly ingesting harmful chemicals by licking her paws afterward.

More dogs become lost during winter months because the cold and snowy weather makes it easier for them to lose their scent and become disoriented. Play it safe and be cautious about letting your dog off leash unless you know you can keep track of her.

Avoid leaving your dog in a parked car in frigid weather. The vehicle's interior can quickly become ice cold, causing hypothermia. Hardy, cold-weather breeds like huskies or malamutes should be fine for short periods if they have blankets and bedding to keep them warm. But it's best to avoid leaving them, as you have no way of knowing if you'll be delayed.

Encounters with Aggressive Dogs

People who've had run-ins with aggressive dogs while out walking their own dog often say the same thing: that the dog "came out of nowhere" and attacked them or their dog without provocation. To avoid a dangerous encounter while out walking, always be aware of your surroundings. Don't jabber away on your cell phone or have your music cranked up on headphones. Keep an eye out for open garages, open gates, alleys, and other places an aggressive dog can bolt from. If you see these things up ahead, cross over to the other side of the street. If you notice an aggressive-looking dog in the distance, get your dog out of its sight by turning a corner, ducking behind a parked car, or placing toy-size dogs under your shirt. If you live in a neighborhood notorious for aggressive dogs, drive to a better location to take your walk.

Should the worst happen and you or your dog is attacked without warning, the first thing to do is *drop the leash*. Otherwise you'll all get tangled up together, exacerbating the problem. Dropping the leash will also give larger dogs a chance to defend themselves, and give smaller dogs an opportunity to run away.
If an aggressive dog threatens your personal safety, the following tips can help:

- Never run away or scream. This can encourage the dog to chase you down. If you see an able-bodied person nearby, calmly call out to them for assistance.

- "Be a Tree"—stand quiet and still with your hands at your sides and don't look the dog directly in the eye, which can be interpreted as a challenge. Act calm and unafraid. If the dog continues threatening you, say, "No!" with a firm voice and slowly take a few steps backward, then continue backing away to a safe place.

- Scan your immediate area for a stick, rock, trash-can lid, or anything you can use to defend yourself if necessary.

- Take your jacket, sweater, purse, backpack—whatever you have with you, and "feed" it to the dog if he lunges at you.

- If you are knocked to the ground, curl into a ball with your hands over your ears to protect your head, neck, and stomach. If you have a small dog, try to shield her underneath you.

BREAKING UP A DOG FIGHT

Dog fights are always unpredictable. While many minor squabbles resolve themselves in a few seconds without any human intervention, true dog fights, where one or both dogs are viciously biting, are serious business. Attempting to break up a fight involves risking your own safety, since dogs in attack mode are operating on instinct and may not react rationally to human intervention—even if they're normally not aggressive toward people. If you're prepared to assume the risk, here are some helpful tips recommended by trainers and veterinarians:

- Avoid screaming. Never hit or strike a dog.

- Don't place your body in between two dogs in a fight or attempt to grab the collars. Keep your hands away from the dogs' mouths and faces.

- If outdoors, use a garden hose or bucket of water to douse and startle the dogs. Aim for the face of the most aggressive dog. An air horn can also create an effective distraction.

- If indoors, wedge a chair, broomstick, or other large item between the dogs to physically separate them.

- If there is another person to help you, lift the hind legs of each dog and pull them apart in a backward motion. This action will throw off their balance and make them more likely to let go of each other. If alone, you can attempt to grab the hind legs of the most aggressive dog and pull him away.

- Once separated, lasso each dog with a leash and take them out of sight of each other as quickly as possible. Using a muzzle if necessary, carefully inspect the dogs for injuries (see page 129 for how to treat bite wounds).

Happy Trails: Travel and Adventure with Your Dog

One of the great things about dogs is their willingness to do just about anything with you. From a day at the beach to a trip to the dry cleaner, it's all fun and games to your faithful buddy. But this doesn't mean you should just throw your dog in the car and take off on a whim. Some forethought is necessary, and there may be times when it's best to leave her home for her own protection (such as very hot weather or large crowds). In most cases, a little preparation is all you need for a safe, tail-wagging good time.

ON THE ROAD: DOG SAFETY

When we think of dogs in cars, it's hard not to conjure up the classic image of a smiling dog's head hanging out the window, tongue blowing sideways, slobber flying in the breeze. Those were the good old days. The statistics on dogs being injured or killed while riding in cars—or causing injury to others in the vehicle—are substantial enough that it's crazy not to take precautions.

Rule #1: No Riding Shotgun

Giving a dog free rein inside a moving vehicle is never a good idea. For starters, she can cause an accident by jumping into your lap, bumping the steering wheel, or getting between your feet and the pedals. If you brake suddenly, she can fly forward, causing severe injury to herself, you, or other passengers. If she's riding in the front passenger seat and the airbags deploy, she can be killed by the force of the airbag—which is designed for the height of a much taller human. Or she can jump out the window and be hit by oncoming traffic—dogs have even been known to roll the window down themselves by pushing the button with their paw.

Things are no better riding loose in the back of an open vehicle, where a dog can fall or jump out and quickly get hit before you can save her. Even dogs that are tethered by their leashes are in danger of strangling if they go over the side.

Luckily, there are several ways to safely transport your dog, and a variety of products designed for every type of vehicle. See the Resources section on page 161 for a few recommendations on the following types of equipment.

Kennel. Kennels (also referred to as crates or cages) are considered by many canine professionals to be the safest way to transport a dog. There are many types to choose from, but for car travel, a plastic or soft-sided kennel is preferable. It should be large enough for the dog to sit, stand up, lie down, and turn around. If you have a short-nosed breed like a pug or bulldog, going a size up will ensure she has plenty of air circulation (these breeds can be prone to breathing difficulties).

For larger vehicles such as station wagons and SUVs, the cargo area in the back is the ideal location for the kennel. If you have a smaller dog and the kennel will fit in the backseat, be sure to anchor the sides to prevent it from sliding off the seat.

Weather permitting, the kennel can also be placed in the back of an open truck, provided it's carefully anchored in place on both sides and the dog will be dry, comfortable, and neither too hot nor too cold.

Car Harness. A car harness is a soft, generously proportioned body harness made especially for dogs that attaches to the vehicle's seat belt. Some varieties include a short extension lead that allows the dog a bit more freedom of movement but will still prevent her from climbing into the front seat or flying forward in an accident. **NEVER use a neck collar to restrain a dog while driving—she could choke or suffer throat damage if jerked by sudden braking or a collision.**

A great way to use a car harness with an extension lead is in conjunction with a backseat pet "hammock." These products close the gap between the front and back seats so the dog can't fall on the floor but can still safely move around to reposition herself during longer car rides.

Vehicle Barrier. Vehicle barriers are made to protect human passengers more than dogs, but they're certainly better than nothing. Used in larger vehicles like wagons and SUVs, an adjustable wire partition blocks off the rear of the vehicle to contain the dog and keep her from flying forward in a collision. However, the dog can still be thrown around in the back of the vehicle, making barriers less than ideal.

Rule #2: Never Leave Your Dog Alone in the Car

The number-one cause of fatal heatstroke in dogs comes from being left alone in a parked car—even in mild weather. Studies indicate that in outside temperatures as low as 72°F (22°C), a parked vehicle's interior temperature to can heat up an additional 40°F (22.5°C) within an hour. Cracking the window or parking in the

The soft, generous proportions of a car harness allow your dog to ride both safely and comfortably. Be sure to buckle your dog in the back seat to avoid potential airbag injuries.

shade has little effect. If the sun is out, the risk exists, and humid conditions make these risks even greater. (The dangers of heatstroke are discussed at length on page 97.)

Even if you plan to leave your dog for just a few minutes, there's always the potential of being delayed or distracted by unforeseen circumstances. And rolling the windows down all the way exposes your dog to teasing by strangers and presents the possibility of theft or of your dog jumping out the window.

Rule #3: Bring Supplies

If you frequently take your dog along for the ride, it's wise to keep a few essentials in your vehicle. These include water and a dish, waste bags, a towel, food or treats, an extra leash, and a favorite toy. By doing so, you'll always be prepared for a change of plans or spontaneous adventure.

A few quiet rest stops (along with frequent leg-stretching opportunities) will be much appreciated by your traveling companion during long road trips.

easing the strain of long car rides

When driving long distances, stop frequently to let the dog stretch her legs, relieve herself, drink some water, and if necessary, have a brief play session to alleviate pent-up energy. For young puppies, this could be as often as every half hour, and for adult dogs every few hours or so (provided they've been well exercised before starting the drive). If you're traveling on the weekend and have trouble finding a spot to take a break and toss the ball, you might get lucky pulling off near a large office building or commercial business park. These places are often deserted on the weekends and have large green lawns, not to mention trash cans for your waste bags. If you'll be crossing state lines or international borders, it's a good idea to take a copy of your dog's rabies certificate, just in case.

CAMPING, HIKING, AND WILDERNESS TRIPS

Camping and hiking with your dog is one of life's great pleasures, provided your pooch is well suited to the particular excursion and you've sufficiently prepared for the trip. The most important factor to consider before planning such an outing is whether you truly believe your dog will enjoy herself. Is she well social-ized and confident in new situations? Is she control-lable around other people and pets? Does she bark at or chase birds, squirrels, or other wild animals? Will the weather be too hot or cold to ensure her comfort and safety? Naturally, you can't predict the exact conditions of your adventure. But considering such matters might make you rethink or adjust your plans so everyone has a good time and you're not left to worry about your dog and spoil your trip.

Careful consideration should be given before tak-ing a puppy on a camping or hiking trip. Depending on her age, she may not have all the required vaccines to protect her. The long car ride and climate might be too extreme for her comfort. As for hiking, pup-pies should not be expected to walk long distances, especially uphill. Their growing bodies simply haven't matured enough to engage in adult-dog activities. If you have doubts about whether or not your pup is old enough to accompany you, consult your veterinarian.

BEFORE YOU LEAVE

Check the rules at the campground and/or hiking trails you plan on using to make sure that dogs are al-lowed, or if there are any dog policies you're unwilling or unable to comply with.

Learn about any hazards in the area such as poison-ous snakes, porcupines, disease-carrying ticks, or wa-terborne parasites like giardia (the local forest service

booster vaccine alternative

A titer is a blood test that determines how much immunity your dog has against certain diseases like distemper and parvo. Performing titers can often spare your dog from unnecessary boosters or revaccinating too soon, which many vets believe can jeopardize a dog's health.

or ranger station is usually a good resource). You can prepare in advance for some potential mishaps by taking needle-nose pliers to remove porcupine quills, antihistamine for insect stings, or a sheet or nylon poncho to use as a two-person stretcher to carry a large, injured dog. Make sure these items are in your dog's first-aid kit.

Confirm that your dog is current on her rabies vaccine. If she's due for other booster shots, consider having a titer done first to see if they're really necessary. Make sure your dog is up-to-date on flea, tick, and heartworm prevention, and that her ID tags and microchip information are up-to-date.

Consider canine foot care and outdoor gear. Trim the dog's nails to prevent them from tearing or breaking on rugged trails. If you plan on investing in dog boots, be sure to get your dog used to them first! While these can be useful equipment on rough terrain, many dogs take quite a while to acclimate to the sensation of walking with booties on, and some dogs reject them altogether. Depending on the climate, you may want to bring other outdoor dog gear with you, such as a jacket for cold weather, or a cooling vest or bandanna for hot weather. If you have a light- or pink-skinned dog, pet-safe sunscreen is also a wise purchase. Trimming the hair between their toes and around their ears helps cut down on foxtails and burrs latching on.

Ensure food and water needs are tended to. When packing for the trip, take water from home or bottled water. Do not let your dog drink from streams or lakes, which can cause intestinal upset and the potential for ingesting bacteria or parasites like giardia. Other items to take include food and treats, toys, a collapsible dish, waste bags, a towel, any medications, a brush, first-aid kit, and an extra-long leash in case you need to tether her at your campsite. Decide where the dog will be sleeping and pack accordingly, either with a bed, soft crate, blankets, or the like.

Be sure your dog is in good physical condition. If she doesn't normally hike, she'll need plenty of time to gradually work up to the length and difficulty of the planned outings. Keep in mind, too, that factors like high altitude or extreme weather might affect her ability to keep up with you.

AT YOUR DESTINATION

If you're staying in a rented cabin, **look around for rodent bait and traps**—a common discovery in vacation rentals that sit unused much of the year. Check the closets, kitchen, and hidden corners and remove anything that can harm your dog. If you're camping in the great outdoors, **make sure there's adequate shade and shelter at your site**.

On the trails, **take water and a collapsible dish** and offer it to the dog often to prevent her from drinking from streams and lakes. Beware of heatstroke if it's warm and humid (see page 97 for more on heatstroke). If your dog seems tired or lies down, always let her rest. Some dogs, in their desire to please, will over-exert themselves to keep up with you, so it's up to you to make sure she's not overdoing it.

After your excursion, **give your pooch a once-over, checking her ears, face, body, and feet** for any foxtails, burrs, or ticks she may have picked up along the way. Check her paw pads for cuts, burns, or stickers. Give her a quick brushing to remove the day's dust and pollen. Then give her a well-deserved dinner, belly rub, and a good night's rest. A bedtime story is optional.

travel tip:
emergency vet clinics

When taking your dog along on vacation, plan ahead by obtaining the address and phone number of a local emergency veterinary clinic for your destination—especially if you'll be camping, hiking, or engaging in other outdoor activities where your dog may find herself on the receiving end of an angry porcupine or other unfortunate mishap.

safety tip:
thin ice

While exploring a wintry landscape, carry a cell phone with you and know exactly where you are, and whether there are frozen lakes nearby. Keep your dog leashed at all times around frozen lakes. If the worst happens and your dog falls through thin ice, DO NOT ATTEMPT TO GO AFTER YOUR DOG! A dog can survive longer in freezing water than a human. Call for help, and keep an eye on the dog's location until help arrives.

SNOW TRIPS

Most dogs are an absolute blast to take along on a snow trip. They run, dig, frolic, and catch snowballs in midair. In some locations, a dog can accompany you on cross-country skiing or snowshoeing outings. And of course, they make great companions to curl up near the fireplace with at the end of the day.

As with most activities, a few precautions are necessary to make your dog's snow adventure a safe one.

Before your trip, **check the dog rules at your destination** so you know what to expect. In most public areas, dogs must be leashed, but you can ask the forest service if there are any snow parks or other safe areas where off-leash access is allowed.

Trim your dog's nails and any excess hair between her toes. Long nails can tear in deep snow, and snow that gets stuck between their pads can freeze into painful ice balls. Consider booties if your dog isn't a cold weather breed—just be sure she has a chance to get used to them first. If your dog doesn't take to the booties, protective paw wax can be applied to her pads and between her toes. If she's thin coated, consider getting her a warm sweater. Don't forget to pack the first-aid kit and a few warm blankets.

Cold air and high altitude can make your dog less tolerant to lengthy activity. Sometimes all it takes is one enthusiastic sprint to cause exhaustion. Monitor your dog's energy level and provide her with plenty of water, warmth, and rest when she's had enough. Dogs also tend to burn more calories in the snow, so if her activity level is significantly increased, increase her daily food ration by about 20 to 30 percent.

Avoid letting your dog run loose in deep snow. The ever-changing depth of the terrain beneath is impossible for a dog (or person) to gauge, and sometimes a dog can dislocate a joint by sinking too deep and then jerking a leg out quickly.

Upon returning from a snowy outing, wipe down your dog's feet, legs, and underside to remove any snow or ice, taking special care with the area between the toes. And always be on the lookout for hypothermia and frostbite. (To refresh your memory of these and other cold weather hazards, see page 100.)

BOATING AND BEACH DAYS

A day spent boating or beaching is exciting for many a water-loving canine. To make the planned outing both safe and successful, having the right gear is essential. For any sunny day near the water, you'll need to pack a few basics:

- a travel dish
- a big jug of water
- pet-safe sunscreen (for light-skinned, thin-coated, or pink-nosed pooches)
- float coat (if boating or the dog is an inexperienced swimmer)
- towels
- treats
- waste bags
- water toys

Common sense is a big factor in boating and beach safety. Oftentimes these activities are so relaxing and enjoyable for some people, they tend to be lax in watching the dog to make sure she's getting enough shade, rest, and water.

On the Boat

All dogs, regardless of how well they can swim, should **wear a personal flotation device, or "float coat," while on a boat.** Dogs that fall overboard accidentally can grow fatigued very quickly, especially in strong current, and can drown before you even notice they're missing.

Supervise your dog while on board. Make sure there is adequate shade for her, and ensure that the deck is not too slippery or hot for her to walk on (both common with fiberglass-bottom boats).

If you're on a lake or calm ocean and you plan on letting the dog swim, a doggie boat ladder can be a very useful safety tool. These lightweight ladders can be purchased at marine supply stores and feature a slip-resistant design that makes exiting the water much easier. Combined with the dog's float coat (which has a handle at the top) you'll be able to help the dog out of the water more easily.

If the dog is not a swimmer and you feel you can't supervise her properly, having a boat alarm is a good idea. These work the same way as some pool alarms, where the dog wears a remote collar that sounds an alarm at the base (which you've plugged in on the boat) if the dog falls overboard. These can also be purchased at marine and pool supply stores.

Be very cautious with any fishing gear on the boat. Dogs love to go after fishing tackle (you can hardly blame them—it all smells like fish!) and often get fishhooks caught in their mouths, or worse, swallow them whole.

Keep your dog's first boat outing short. Not all dogs like the unstable motion of boats, and you won't know until you're out on the water. It often helps to bring your dog to the boat an hour before you leave and let her walk around on it. If she's never worn her float coat before, this is also a good time to let her splash around with it on. (Finally, don't forget to let your dog relieve herself prior to casting off!)

At the Beach

On a warm, sunny day, **take a beach umbrella to provide shade for your dog**—especially if she isn't a swimmer and won't be able to cool off in the water. If your dog is used to swimming in a pool but has never been in the surf, **a float coat should be worn** until you're certain she can ride the waves safely on her own. These items, plus the supplies mentioned above (water, dish, sunscreen, towels, toys, etc.) should be all you need for a splashing good time.

Always check the surf conditions before you leave. A strong current or undertow can be extremely dangerous for even the most experienced canine (and human) swimmers, and can pull your dog under or carry her out to sea. When a strong current is present, stick to splashing around in the shallow surf and building sand castles with your dog (you build the castle, she digs the moat). You'll still have a great time and be much safer.

When you get home, **rinse the dog's coat thoroughly** or give her a quick bath to get the itchy salt-water off. If the dog has been swimming in the ocean, don't be alarmed if she has loose stools the next day—swallowing sand and saltwater can do that to a dog. If it persists, however, take her in for a checkup.

Practice with your dog before the flight to make sure she's comfortable spending time in her crate or carrier.

FLYING WITH YOUR DOG

Many people who've flown with their dogs agree that the process can be unpleasant for both their pets and themselves. This is especially true for dogs that must fly below cabin, where the conditions are not only stressful for a dog, they can also be dangerous. This has led some airlines to reexamine their dog policies to make them safer and more comfortable—while other airlines have stopped flying dogs altogether. There is genuine, well-founded concern about flying any short-nosed-breed dog such as a pug, bulldog, or boxer. Many airlines won't fly these breeds due to their already limited respiratory abilities.

Despite all this, there may come a time when flying your dog becomes necessary (for example, if you're moving a far distance away). If your dog is in good health (and not a short-nosed breed) and the airline has reasonable policies and practices regarding pet transportation, you should be able to arrange a successful journey for your dog, provided you take time in advance to prepare.

Booking A Pet-Friendly Flight

Fly direct whenever possible, and choose a flight time to best accommodate your dog's comfort and safety. For example, if it's summer, fly at night when the temperature is cooler (heatstroke is one of the health concerns when flying below cabin). On the other hand, if it's icy cold outside you'll want to book a late-morning or afternoon flight when it will be warmer. Speak to the airline to confirm that the area your dog will be kept in flight is climate controlled and pressurized for your dog's safety. If not, find another airline—it's not worth the risk. Double-check the airline's policies (such as health certificate requirements) to be sure you're clear on everything so there are no snags at the airport.

Preparing the Crate for Air Travel

You'll need to have an airline-approved, appropriately sized crate for your dog. Using markers or bright-colored paint, write your dog's name in big letters across the top of the crate. Write something like "I'm Lucy and I'm very friendly!" to put the baggage handlers at ease. Then type up instructions on a sheet of paper listing your name, flight number(s), your cell phone and emergency contact numbers, and final destination. Tape this on top of the crate next to your dog's name. Attach a small bag of food, extra water and a leash in a pack to the back of the crate.

Prepare the inside of the crate by making sure there are sturdy water and food dishes attached. Place an old shirt with your scent on it inside, along with a kennel pad or other soft bedding. The day before the flight, fill the water dish two-thirds full and freeze it, then take it with you to place in the crate right before you check the dog in, along with a durable, treat-stuffed toy.

Preparing the Dog for Air Travel

The more time you spend getting the dog used to her crate before the trip, the better off she'll be (see page 32 for advice on teaching your dog to enjoy her crate). Practice lifting the crate with the dog inside (you may need someone to help you do this) and gently jostling it around. This will help prepare her for what's to come at the airport.

Your dog will need a health-check certificate from her vet. Be sure you time the vet visit so that the certificate will remain valid for your return flight. If you feel it's necessary, now is also the time to speak with your veterinarian about the possibility of *lightly* sedating your dog for the flight, either with a natural remedy or a prescription. This practice has become quite controversial in the veterinary community, as many believe it can jeopardize pets' safety by affecting their respiratory function below cabin. Other vets believe it's not realistic to expect a dog to endure the stress of a flight without light sedation. This should be a carefully considered decision based on your dog's health, breed, and circumstances of travel, and made only with the full approval of your veterinarian.

Purchase a fabric or nylon snap-buckle or break-away collar for the flight and write your dog's information right on the collar. Do not attach any tags to the collar or use any chain or prong collars, which can get caught in the wire crate door.

On the day of the flight, give your dog plenty of exercise but allow sufficient time for her to drink water and pass it before you leave the house. Adjust her feeding schedule so that you don't anticipate her needing to relieve herself during the flight. Do not feed her within two hours of departure.

Arriving at the Airport

Arrive early and take your dog for a long walk to stretch her legs and relieve herself again. Be confident, calm, and happy when you bid her farewell, and check the airline tags on her crate to make sure they're accurate. Remind every airline employee you deal with at check-in and the gate that you are traveling with a dog and confirm the location where you'll pick her up upon landing.

sweet-talking the flight crew

A trick recommended by a seasoned airline pilot: bring two packets of goodies (such as a sealed box of chocolates wrapped in clear cellophane) on board, a photo of your dog, and a note that says "Dear Captain, Please know that on this flight, you are carrying the most precious cargo in the world, my beloved dog [insert name]. Please confirm she is on board and that her area is safely pressurized and climate controlled. She means the world to our family and we appreciate your kindness." Give one package of goodies to the flight crew and ask your flight attendant to deliver the other package with the note and photo of your dog to the cockpit.

Leaving Your Dog in the Care of Others

There will be times when you need to leave your dog in someone else's care. Whether it's for a day, a week, or longer, you'll want to find the perfect person or facility to entrust with your precious pooch.

First consider what situation is best for the type of dog you have. Elderly dogs, young puppies, dogs with medical conditions, or those that are fearful or not well socialized are best left in their home environment with a professional pet sitter, or in the home of a trusted friend or relative. However, if your dog is healthy, active, and social, you have the option of kennels and boarding facilities.

CHOOSING A PET SITTER

To begin your search for a pet sitter, consider asking friends, neighbors, or your veterinarian for recommendations. Having a reference from someone you know will help you feel at ease as you plan for time apart from your dog. You can also look for postings at your local pet store or access pet sitting directories online. (See Resources, page 157, for a list of professional pet sitter organizations.)

First, schedule a phone interview. A simple conversation can tell you a lot about a potential pet sitter's attitude and personality, and whether you'll feel comfortable having her in your home. Discuss her rates, experience, training, references, and professional affiliations. Ask how much time she'll be spending with

your dog and other pets, and whether she performs house-sitting tasks such as taking in the mail or watering plants. A pet sitter who provides a written service contract and questionnaire to learn details about your dog is preferable. Ideally, she should also be bonded and insured.

After the interview, invite the pet sitter to your home to see how well she interacts with your dog. Show her the dog's daily routine. Take the dog for a walk together and review any commands or habits the sitter should be aware of. Teach house rules the dog must follow and games the dog enjoys. The more you can show the pet sitter how to maintain consistency in your dog's routine, the greater chance the dog will be comfortable while you're away.

Before hiring the sitter, exchange mobile phone and email information. Review logistics in your home such as where you keep the dog's food, supplies, and any medications, as well as locks, gates, alarm codes, circuit breaker location, and so on.

Be Organized Before Your Trip

The dog's collar and ID tags should be securely in place. Leave detailed, written instructions, including information about where you'll be staying, travel itinerary, emergency contact numbers, your veterinarian's information, microchip details, and any medical information. All supplies should be together in a predetermined place. Agree on the exact time the sitter will begin and end her services, and make sure she confirms your safe arrival home.

It is wise to establish a backup plan should anything prevent your pet sitter from being able to fulfill her duties, such as car trouble, an illness, or the like. Entrust a neighbor with a house key and be sure the neighbor and sitter share contact information.

While away, you may understandably have the urge to call the pet sitter to see how your dog is doing. Scheduling a few mutually convenient times for a check-in can save you from playing phone tag and disrupting your trip. You may also want to schedule a follow-up conversation upon your return to learn how the experience was for the sitter as well as your dog and other pets.

A young puppy needs the constant love, presence, and consistency of her new family. Avoid taking trips without her until she's about 6 months old, unless it's absolutely necessary.

CHOOSING A KENNEL OR BOARDING FACILITY

If there is a boarding facility in your area and the rates are in your budget, investigate your options before you commit. While most places are safe and well run, others can be poorly staffed and chaotic.

Interview the staff. Is the facility run by experienced dog professionals? Ask about the training and skills of the kennel employees. The level of enthusiasm shown by the staff should make you feel at ease about leaving your dog there.

Expect high standards. A reputable facility will want to meet your dog before her stay, to make sure she's friendly, healthy, and socialized. They should require proof of up-to-date vaccines or titers, and a current Bordetella (kennel cough) vaccine. Many will require a questionnaire about your dog and her medical history, habits, likes, and dislikes.

Also, tour the facility to see the areas your dog will have access to. The overall impression should be one of cleanliness and organization.

Learn their safety policies. Is there someone on the premises 24/7 in case of emergency? Does the staff have training in pet first aid? How far away is the nearest emergency hospital? What are their procedures if your dog were to need aid? Basic safety policy questions should be easily answered by any staff member.

Observe the grounds and play surfaces. Where will your dog be relieving herself? Many dogs have no experience with artificial grass, concrete, gravel, or other surfaces, and could have difficulty relieving themselves in certain areas they may be kept in. Keep in mind, the paw pads of dogs that don't get a lot of outdoor activity paw pads may be susceptible to cuts and tears from running around on pavement—minor injuries that will heal with basic first aid.

Ask about the play and exercise routine. How much daily playtime or exercise will your dog receive? If the facility is cage-free, how do they screen the dogs to ensure compatibility? Are there separate areas for big and small dogs? If there will be group play, schedule a play session before leaving your dog to ensure she's comfortable in this type of setting.

If the facility is one in which your dog will have her own private kennel, how much time will the dog spend outside her kennel each day? Is there one-on-one play time? How long will the daily walks be?

Finally, keep in mind that for many dogs that aren't regularly boarded, their experience away at "camp" can be as exhausting as it is exhilarating. Don't be surprised if your dog needs lots of extra sleep for a couple of days afterwards.

Supply your dog's own food, if possible. Keeping your dog on her regular diet is always preferable, to avoid any digestive upset from a sudden change in diet.

Understand the drop off, pick-up, and payment policies. If there's an overnight boarding rate, find out how they calculate the final pick up day. Are there extra fees for baths, playtime, or to give medications? Understand all the costs up front so there are no surprises.

Finally, have a safe and enjoyable trip, knowing your dog is in capable hands.

five

EMERGENCY FIRST AID

True life-threatening emergencies are few and far between. But should such an accident ever happen to your dog, you are most likely the one who will reach him first, and every second counts. It's up to you to take action right away—and let's be realistic—you might not have this book or another first-aid guide at your fingertips when you need it. Learning to perform a few emergency first-aid techniques *before* something happens will help prepare you if that time ever comes. It will also make referring to this chapter much easier in a stressful situation.

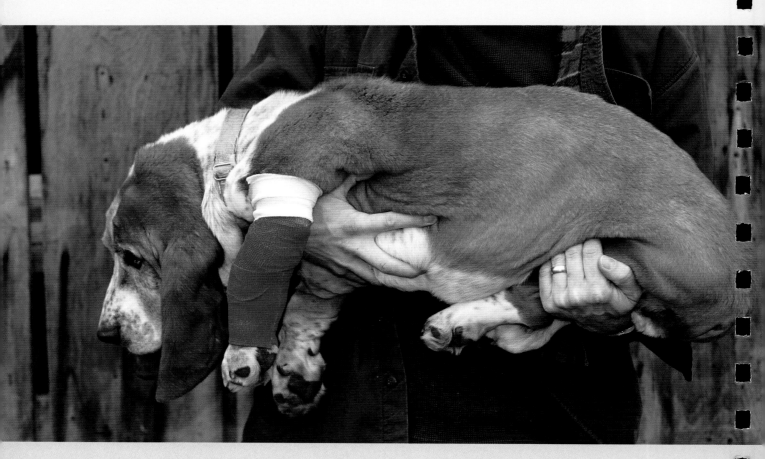

Included here are essential first-aid techniques and when to use them, plus a treatment guide to some of the most common life-threatening situations. It is by no means a complete first-aid guide for dogs. By focusing on the basics such as reading vital signs, how to restrain an injured dog, CPR, the canine Heimlich maneuver, treating shock, and safe transportation techniques, you can adapt these skills to dozens of serious situations, buying your dog precious time until professional help takes over—and perhaps even saving his life.

Basic First-Aid Techniques

Learning and practicing basic canine first aid can give you the confidence and ability to help your dog in an emergency. This section will walk you through the moves, but *hands-on training is highly recommended* for mastering them. Ask your veterinarian, local Red Cross, or major pet store chain for information on pet first-aid classes in your area. If none are available, taking a human first aid/CPR course is the next best thing, since there are many similarities in treating people and pets. There are also excellent pet first-aid videos and online classes available, which you'll find listed in the Resources section on page 157.

LOOK, ASSESS, AND RESPOND

The first rule in any emergency is to look, assess, and respond. **Look** at the scene before you rush in, to determine what has happened and whether it's safe to approach. For example, has the dog been hit by a car, and is it safe to go into the street after him? Once you've safely reached the dog and determined what's happened, the next step is to **assess** the dog's injuries. For example, is he bleeding? Unconscious? By assessing the dog's vital signs and/or injuries, you will then know how to **respond**. For example, if the dog isn't breathing, you'll respond by performing rescue breathing. If he has no heartbeat or pulse, you'll respond by performing CPR. If he has broken bones, you'll respond by stabilizing him for transport. Whenever in doubt, call a vet for help and focus on getting emergency treatment as quickly as possible.

Restraining a Dog for Treatment

To properly treat an injured dog, you'll need to restrain him to prevent him from fleeing. Since even the friendliest dog can bite when scared or in pain, in some cases you may also need to muzzle him, for your own protection as well as the dog's.

Step 1: Approach Calmly

Approach the dog slowly, speaking in a calm, low voice. Let him see what you're doing, and don't make any big, sudden movements. If the dog doesn't know you, allow him to sniff the back of your hand. Do not stare directly into the dog's eyes—this can be intimidating.

Step 2: Prevent Fleeing

If possible, use a standard, 6-foot leash to prevent the dog from fleeing. Make a loop in the leash by passing the metal clasp end through the handle, then slip it over the dog's head. You may need to do this from behind or from the side. Note: Skip this step if the dog has a throat or neck injury.

Step 3: Muzzle the Dog If Necessary

If you have a commercial dog muzzle, put it on according to directions. Otherwise, use a necktie, length of gauze, panty hose, or strip of fabric approximately 24 to 36 inches (61 to 91.4 cm) long. You can even improvise with a belt or leash as a last resort.

For short-nosed breeds such as bulldogs, pugs, or boxers, there is not enough snout length to use a traditional muzzle. Instead, use a muzzle specially made for these breeds, or you can slip a pillowcase over the head and hold it loosely at the neck. Alternatively, you can cover the head with a bath towel—just be sure not to block respiration.

Make a knot in the center of the material. (This will help anchor the muzzle under the dog's chin.) Next, tie a half-knot in the material to create a loop, and slip it over the dog's snout with the half-knot on top. Tighten snugly, but not so tight that you restrict the dog's breathing.

Bring the two ends of the material down along the sides of the snout and cross them under the chin.

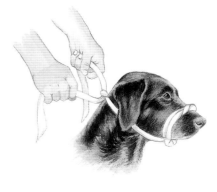

Draw the ends back under the ears, and tie a bow at the back of the head.

Step 4: Restrain for Treatment

Choosing the best method of restraint depends on the type of injury you're treating. Use the method that causes the least pressure and the best accessibility to the injured area. For small and medium-size dogs, placing them on a table will help prevent them from fleeing.

One-Person Restraint Method

If there is no one to help you, your best bet is to muzzle the dog as described above, attach a leash to his collar, and tie the leash to a sturdy object with minimal slack. If all else fails or the injury prevents you from tying him up, try getting the dog into a tight space such as a laundry room or small bathroom to work on him.

Note: Never muzzle a dog that is vomiting, coughing, unconscious, or has difficulty breathing, seizures, or a jaw/mouth injury.

Two-Person Restraint Methods (one person restrains, the other treats the dog)

Head/Hug Method: *Wrap one arm under and around the dog's neck. Place the other arm under his belly and wrap around the side of the chest. Hug the dog against your chest for stability.*

Kneeling Restraint: *This method is best for small dogs or dogs with prominent eyes (which can pop out of their sockets if the neck is restrained too tightly). Kneel down and hold the dog between your legs, facing outward. Cup your hands under the chin and on top of the head to hold the dog steady for treatment.*

Lying Dog on Side (Step 1): *Stand facing the side of the dog, bend over, and grab on to the front and rear legs that are closest to your body.*

Lying Dog on Side (Step 2): *Bending your knees, lift the dog's legs up and toward you. Slowly lower the dog down onto his side, taking care to not bang his head or body on the floor. Continue holding the legs, pressing your forearms on top of the dog's body to hold him in place.*

IS IT SAFE TO TAKE ACTION?

You love your dog, and your instinct may be to rush to his aid or the aid of another dog no matter what the circumstances. But you can't help the dog if you kill yourself in the process! Stay calm and assess the situation before taking action. For example:

- Never rush into moving traffic to rescue a dog that's been hit by a car. Instead, wave your arms to signal cars to stop before proceeding.

- Don't place your body in between two dogs in a fight, or attempt to grab the collars. Keep your hands away from the dogs' face and mouth area. For strategies on how to break up a dog fight, see page 102.

- Do not attempt to rescue a dog that has fallen through thin ice unless you can do so without falling in yourself. A dog can survive much longer than a person in frigid water. Call for help. Similarly, do not attempt to rescue a drowning dog in dangerous current or in any water if you are not a strong swimmer.

- Never touch a dog that has suffered electric shock and is still in contact with the electric cord until you've turned off the power, or you could be electrocuted yourself. Use a nonconductive item like a wooden broomstick or chair to move the dog away from the power source, throw the breaker switch, or unplug the cord while wearing rubber gloves before attempting first aid.

CAUTION: AGGRESSION IN AN INJURED DOG

You should not attempt to treat a strange, aggressive dog. Instead, keep track of his location and call your local animal shelter or animal control for assistance if the dog exhibits the following signs:

- Growling, snarling, snapping, lunging, hair along the neck and back (hackles) up

- Ears forward with tail raised high

- Ears pinned back tight to the head, with tail tucked between legs while snarling and hackles are up

Rescue Breathing and CPR

If a dog is unconscious and has stopped breathing, you must react immediately. You have only a few minutes to attempt to save him by beginning rescue breathing (artificial respiration) and if necessary, CPR (rescue breathing combined with chest compressions). Summon help if possible. CPR can be performed on the way to the animal hospital, if there is someone available to drive.

The ABC's of CPR

When administering CPR to a dog, an easy method to help you remember the steps described in this section is the ABCs: airway, breathing, circulation. Airway: Make sure the dog's airway is open and clear of obstructions. Breathing: Check to see if the dog is breathing and begin rescue breathing if necessary. Circulation: Check for a heartbeat or pulse and begin chest compressions (CPR) if necessary.

The first thing you must do is make sure the dog is definitely unconscious before beginning rescue breathing/CPR. Speak calmly and try to rouse him by gently shaking his body. If he does not respond:

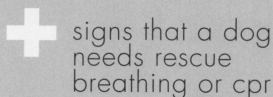

signs that a dog needs rescue breathing or cpr

- Dog is unconscious AND not breathing
- Dog has no pulse or heartbeat

Note: An unconscious dog can still be breathing and have a heartbeat. Never perform rescue breathing without confirming the dog has stopped breathing, and never perform CPR without confirming the dog's heart has stopped.

Step 1: Open the Airway

With the dog lying on his right side, tilt the head back slightly to align with the neck and create a more open airway. Pull the tongue forward to the front teeth, look inside the mouth, and check for visible blockages. If necessary, use your finger to sweep the mouth clear of any vomit or foreign matter. If the dog is choking and you can't pull the object out, use the Heimlich maneuver (see Canine Heimlich Maneuver, page 126). **Do not stick your finger deep into the throat unless you clearly see a foreign object.** All dogs have a smooth, bone-like structure (essentially the Adam's apple) located deep in the throat at the base of the tongue, and serious injury could result in mistaking this for a foreign object. As soon as the airway is open:

Step 2: Check for Breathing

Watch for the dog's chest to rise and fall, or place your cheek close to the dog's nose and mouth to feel or listen for breath. If you have a tissue you can hold it in front of the nose and mouth to see if it moves. If the dog is breathing, make him comfortable and proceed to the emergency hospital for treatment. **If he is NOT breathing:**

Step 3: Begin Rescue Breathing

Lean down toward the dog and tilt his head slightly, keeping the head and neck aligned. Hold the mouth tightly closed, and seal your mouth over his nostrils (for a smaller dog, your mouth will naturally seal over the mouth and nose). Exhale firmly, watching for the chest to expand to the point you would see with a normal breath. (Be careful not to over-inflate the lungs.) Give 4 or 5 breaths, waiting for the lungs to deflate completely in between breaths.

Tilt the head slightly while keeping the head and neck aligned. Clasp the mouth firmly shut, then seal your mouth over the dog's nostrils (for smaller dogs, your mouth will naturally seal over both the mouth and nose). Exhale just hard enough for the chest to begin to rise.

If the dog revives: If, after giving the dog 4 or 5 breaths, the dog continues to breathe without assistance, proceed directly to the veterinarian for further treatment.

If breathing continues but is weak and irregular and the dog is still unconscious, continue rescue breathing as someone drives you to the ER. Give approximately 20 breaths per minute.

If the dog is not breathing after 4 or 5 rescue breaths, continue rescue breathing and check for a pulse (figure 1) or heartbeat (figure 2). **If no pulse or heartbeat is present:**

Figure 1 To check for a pulse, press two fingers on the inside of either back leg, at the point where the leg meets the groin area, and feel for a pulsing sensation.

Figure 2 To feel for a heartbeat, lay the dog down on his right side. Bend his front left elbow toward the chest and place your hand at the point on his body where the elbow meets the chest.

Perform CPR

If the dog has no pulse or heartbeat, his heart has stopped and you must immediately begin chest compressions to get blood moving through the body. You will combine these compressions with rescue breathing.

For puppies and dogs under 30 pounds (about 14 kg):

Step 1:

Lay the dog down on his right side on the floor, or a table, facing you.

Step 2:

Cup your hands around the ribcage—the top hand over the point where the left elbow meets the chest, the bottom hand underneath the dog on his right side.

Step 3:

Begin gentle, rapid compressions with your top hand so that the chest moves about ½ to 1 inch (1.3 to 2.5 cm) with each thrust. **Do 15 compressions, and then give 1 breath. Check for a pulse.** If no pulse is detected:

Step 4:

Continue this pattern (15 compressions, then 1 breath), aiming for 80 to 100 compressions per minute. Check for a pulse every 3 to 4 cycles (about once per minute).

Step 5:

CPR should be continued uninterrupted until the dog regains a strong pulse, heartbeat and breathing; you reach the veterinary hospital and professional help takes over; you become too exhausted to continue; or more than 20 minutes have lapsed without a positive outcome.

For dogs over 30 pounds (about 14 kg):

Step 1:

Lay the dog on his right side and kneel facing his back.

Step 2:

Locate the heart by bending the dog's left front elbow towards the chest. The point on his body where the elbow meets the chest is where you will place your hands for compressions.

Step 3:

Straighten your arms and cup one hand over the back of the other, and begin rapid compressions, firm enough so the dog's chest moves about 1 to 3 inches (2.5 to 7.6 cm) with each compression. **Do 15 compressions, and then give 1 breath. Check for a pulse.** If no pulse is detected:

Step 4:

Continue this pattern (15 compressions, then 1 breath), aiming for 80 to100 compressions per minute. Check for a pulse every 3 to 4 cycles (about once per minute).

Step 5:

CPR should be continued uninterrupted until the dog regains a strong pulse, heartbeat and breathing; you reach the veterinary hospital and professional help takes over; you become too exhausted to continue; or more than 20 minutes have lapsed without a positive outcome.

CPR should be performed on the way to the veterinary hospital, if there is someone available to drive.

For a small dog, lay him on his right side, either on the floor, table, or in your lap, with your hands cupped around the ribcage. Gently perform rapid compressions over the heart, taking care not to compress the chest more than an inch or so.

For a dog more than 30 pounds (about 14 kg), lay him on his right side on the floor (if possible, place a soft pillow under his ribcage), and alternate 15 chest compressions with 1 breath. Using the heel of your hand to apply pressure helps you to give a firmer compression.

Keep in mind that CPR is often unsuccessful, even when performed by a veterinarian. If the dog does not survive, remember that you did all you could to help an animal in need.

determining normal vital signs

Preparing in Advance

Practice reading your dog's heart and pulse rate, respiratory rate, and other vital signs regularly so you'll be familiar with how to do it in a stressful situation. See Part 1, page 15 for complete instructions.

NORMAL RESPIRATORY (BREATHING) RATES

Dogs up to 30 lb. (13.6 kg)	10 to 30 breaths per minute/up to 200 pants per minute
Dogs over 30 lb. (13.6 kg)	10 to 30 breaths per minute/up to 200 pants per minute
Puppies	15 to 40 breaths per minute/up to 200 pants per minute

NORMAL HEART RATES

Dogs up to 30 lb (13.6 kg)	100 to 160 beats per minute
Dogs over 30 lb (13.6 kg)	60 to 100 beats per minute
Puppies up to 1 year old	120 to 160 beats per minute

Canine Heimlich Maneuver

This procedure is similar to the Heimlich maneuver for people and is used when a dog's airway is either partially or fully blocked by a stuck object such as a ball, toy, or bone. Before performing the Heimlich maneuver, open the dog's mouth and check to see if the object can be pulled out manually. Pull the tongue forward between the front teeth and use your fingers, tweezers, or forceps/hemostat to grab the object, if possible. Be careful not to push the object further down the throat, and be careful not to get bitten. If unsuccessful, perform the Heimlich maneuver as follows.

For medium to large dogs: Stand behind the dog and put your arms around his waist. Make a fist with your hand, clasp your other hand over it, and place them in the soft spot just under the bottom of the ribcage. Quickly thrust inward and upward 3 to 5 times, then check to see if the object has dislodged.

For small dogs: Pick up the dog and hug him facing outward against your stomach. Wrap one arm around his upper abdomen and make a fist just below his ribcage. Grab your fist with your other hand and thrust inward and upward 3 to 5 times, then check to see if the object has dislodged.

If the dog is unconscious, the Heimlich maneuver can be performed with the dog lying on his side.

Heimlich Maneuver

Wrap your arms around the dog's waist and grab your fist. Place your thumbs against the soft spot just beneath the ribcage and thrust inward and upward.

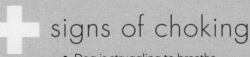

✚ signs of choking

- Dog is struggling to breathe
- Dog is agitated and panicked
- Breathing noises are wheezing and strained
- Gum color turns blue or white

How to Induce Vomiting

If your dog has ingested a toxic substance, in many cases you will need to induce vomiting. To determine whether this is the safe course of action, you must *always* check first by calling your veterinarian or poison control hotline. This is because in some instances, making your dog vomit can do more harm than good. Examples of when NOT to induce vomiting are

- if the toxic substance is caustic (such as bleach or harsh cleansers);
- if the substance is sharp (such as rocks, needles, or bone shards); and
- if the dog shows signs of lethargy, convulsions, difficulty breathing, seizures, shock, uncoordination, or unconsciousness.

It is also important to know that inducing vomiting only buys you a little time until you can get your dog to the vet. It is **by no means** a permanent solution in treating an ingested poison.

Once a vet determines it's prudent to make your dog vomit, administer an oral dose of 3 percent hydrogen peroxide, which can be purchased at your local drugstore, following the dosage guidelines below. You can give it to the dog "straight" using an oral syringe or turkey baster, or mix it with a small amount of milk in a saucer and see if the dog will drink it willingly. Be ready for the dog to vomit soon after. If the dog does not vomit within 15 minutes, you can repeat the procedure up to 3 times, waiting 15 minutes in between each dose, as you make your way to the veterinary hospital.

Note: Syrup of ipecac can be dangerous to dogs and is no longer advised as a method of inducing vomiting.

To induce vomiting, give 1 to 2 teaspoons (5 to 10 ml) of 3 percent hydrogen peroxide for every 10 pounds (5 kg) of body weight, or 1 tablespoon (15 ml) for every 20 pounds (9 kg) of body weight.

Safe Transportation to the Vet

A sick or injured dog can be transported to the vet in many different ways, but the goal is always the same: Create the least discomfort for the dog without causing further damage to the injured area. The best-case scenario is when the dog is still able to walk normally, in which case he can lie in the most comfortable position as you drive to the vet, using a pet carrier, crate, or seat-belt harness—as long as it doesn't restrict the dog in a harmful way.

Carrying an Unconscious or Minimally Injured Dog

If the dog has collapsed, is unconscious, or can't walk on his own and does not have a spinal injury, you will need to carry him to the car. For small dogs, cradle them in your arms as you normally would, taking care to support their upper and lower body while holding them securely to your chest. For medium to large dogs, place one arm around the chest and the other arm wrapped around their hind legs under the rump.

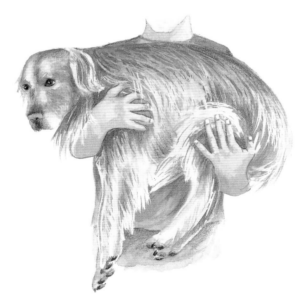

Wrap your arms around the chest and under the rump, as shown. If the hind legs are injured or the dog is limping, wrap one arm around the chest and the other under the belly.

Transporting a Critically Injured Dog

For a dog with suspected injuries to the back, ribcage, or internal organs (from a fall or car accident, for example), immobilize him on a rigid surface like a wooden plank or ironing board, or a removable shelf.

If the dog is lying down, transport him in the same position you found him. Set the rigid surface on the ground along the backside of the dog. Slip your hands underneath the dog's shoulders and hips and gently slide the dog back-first onto the board. Use long strips of fabric, gauze, or rope to secure the dog to the board. Depending on the size of the dog/board, you may need someone to help you lift and carry it to the car.

Note: **If you suspect a chest or lung injury,** transport the dog with the injured side down on the board, leaving the uninjured lung facing up to aid breathing and maintain oxygen flow to the brain. Remove or loosen the dog's collar.

Carefully slide the dog back-first onto the board. Wrap several strips of fabric, gauze, or rope around the board and the dog and tie to secure. If tape is used to tie down the dog, be sure to lay a towel or shirt over the dog first to prevent sticking.

If All Else Fails, Make a Stretcher

If no rigid surface is available or the dog is too large for one person to carry, you can use a thick blanket, towel, shirt, or sheet to create a "stretcher." You will need someone to carry the other end, and ride in the car with you if possible, to prevent the dog from moving and further injuring himself.

If you suspect a head injury, keep the dog's head higher than the body while transporting. This will prevent extra blood from rushing to the head and increasing pressure inside the skull.

Every injury and situation is different. You will likely need to do some improvising to safely transport a seriously injured dog, using pillows, blankets, and the help of others to keep the dog as supported and comfortable as the injury will allow. For less-injured dogs, use a pet carrier or crate whenever possible to help keep them immobilized. And as hard as it may be, try to remain as calm as possible. Your ability to stay calm and in control will help reduce stress in a dog that is already traumatized.

✚ treating shock

A dog that has suffered serious trauma, injury, or blood loss is at risk of going into shock. While transporting such a dog to the hospital, control bleeding by applying direct pressure with a clean cloth, sanitary pad, or bandage; cover him with a warm blanket; and elevate his hind end slightly, but only if there is no evidence of back or spinal injury and it does not cause the dog discomfort. For more information about the symptoms and treatment of shock, see page 147.

Bleeding

Deep wounds, cuts, and lacerations that bleed heavily and do not stop after 5 minutes of direct pressure are serious emergencies requiring immediate treatment. Priority one is to stop the bleeding. Severed arteries are the most serious, and can be identified by rhythmically spurting, bright red blood. Severed veins tend to flow more slowly with darker-colored red blood and are less critical than severed arteries since blood loss happens more slowly. In any case of heavy bleeding, do not try to wash the wound—this could prevent the blood from clotting.

APPLY DIRECT PRESSURE

If possible, wash your hands, use hand sanitizer, or don latex gloves before touching the wound. Apply direct pressure to the wound with a clean washcloth, sanitary napkin, dish towel, nonstick gauze pad, paper towels, or any clean material. Hold for 5 minutes. If the bleeding stops, **do not remove the bandage**—secure it by wrapping gauze or other material around it and proceed to the vet for further treatment.

If the bandage becomes soaked through with blood, do not replace it with another bandage. Instead, place another bandage over it, repeating as necessary, and continue applying pressure. If the blood still seems to be spurting after 5 minutes and you have another set of hands to help you, have that person apply pressure to the area just above the wound while you continue with the direct pressure, which may help stop the flow of blood. If this doesn't help after a minute, the next step is to apply a pressure bandage.

APPLY A PRESSURE BANDAGE

Use a roll of gauze, strip of fabric, elastic bandage, plastic wrap, or tape and wrap it snugly around the bandage several times to create pressure. Make the pressure snug but not overly tight—you should be able to lift up the edge of the wrapping without too much resistance. If the pressure bandage is on a limb and the area below the dressing begins to swell or feel cold to the touch, it is too tight. Rewrap the bandage a bit looser, then secure with tape if possible. Proceed immediately to the veterinary hospital.

ELEVATE THE BLEEDING AREA IF POSSIBLE

If the wound is on a limb or other area that **does not** appear to have broken bones, elevate the body part above the heart if possible, while continuing to apply direct pressure. This will help reduce blood flow to the area. Skip this if doing so puts the dog in greater pain.

treating bite wounds

Bite or puncture wounds, even if they are not bleeding much, are at a high risk of infection. Wash hands thoroughly before treating the dog. Clip the hair around the wound if necessary and carefully wash with sterile saline or antiseptic solution. Seek prompt veterinary treatment, as the dog may need antibiotics to guard against infection.

USE PRESSURE POINTS TO CONTROL BLEEDING

If blood continues to flow or spurt heavily, it may be possible to control the bleeding by pressing on certain points of the dog's body near the wounded area, where the arterial veins run close under the skin.

Use the illustration below to locate the correct pressure point, then apply firm, steady pressure using 3 fingers. Release the pressure slightly for a few seconds every 7 to 10 minutes until you reach the hospital and professional help takes over.

A For bleeding at the head, apply pressure between the lower jaw and ear on the same side where the bleeding is (jugular vein).

B For bleeding at the neck, apply pressure in the soft indentation next to the windpipe, on the same side of the neck where the bleeding is, *below* the wound. Be careful not to press the windpipe and interfere with breathing.

C For a bleeding front leg, apply pressure to the vein located in the "armpit" of the bleeding limb.

D For a bleeding back leg, apply pressure on the inner thigh of the wounded leg, just below the area where the thigh meets the groin.

E For a bleeding tail, lift the dog's tail and apply pressure to the underside of the tail at the base, just above the anus.

DIAGRAM OF PRESSURE POINTS

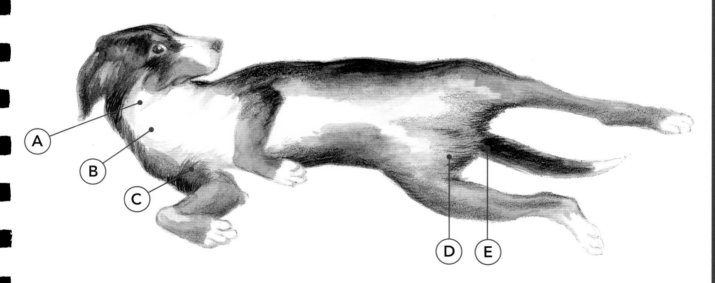

BEWARE OF SHOCK

Heavy blood loss can cause a dog to go into shock, a life-threatening condition that slows oxygen supply to the internal organs. All cases of shock require *immediate treatment*. Watch any heavily bleeding dog for signs of shock and take preventive measures such as wrapping him in a warm blanket and being prepared to perform artificial respiration/CPR if necessary.

INTERNAL BLEEDING

Dogs that have been hit by a car, suffered a bad fall, or ingested certain poisons like rat bait are all at risk for internal bleeding, an emergency requiring immediate veterinary treatment. Signs of internal bleeding are

- pale gums or mucous membranes;
- cool limbs;
- low body temperature;
- bleeding from the ears, nose, mouth, or rectum;
- weakness or agitation; and
- rapid heart rate or breathing.

If you suspect internal bleeding in a dog, treat for shock and head straight to the vet.

See Shock, page 147, for more information.

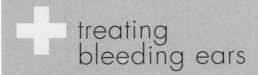

treating bleeding ears

Cuts on dogs' ears tend to bleed a lot and often look more serious than they really are. To stop the bleeding, place a gauze bandage or sanitary pad over the cut and another on the other side of the ear and apply pressure for several minutes. Then, without removing the bandages, fold the ear up against the dog's head and secure in place by wrapping a length of gauze, fabric, or panty hose around the dog's head going over the ear, around the top of the head and under the dog's chin. **Be sure you do not wrap it too tight or interfere with the dog's ability to breathe!** You should be able to slip 2 fingers between the bandage and his chin. Take the dog to a vet the same day, or within 24 hours.

Bloat

Canine bloat is a life-threatening condition in which a dog's stomach twists or rotates, causing air, gas, or food to become trapped inside. *The first and most important priority for any dog with signs of bloat is to get veterinary help as soon as possible.*

TREATMENT FOR BLOAT

- **Seek immediate veterinary treatment** if the dog shows any of the signs listed here. If possible, call the animal hospital while transporting your dog to alert them of your arrival.

- **Beware of shock.** Cover the dog with a blanket as you transport him to the nearest animal hospital. Loosen his collar. If possible, lay a folded towel under his hind end to elevate it slightly. (See Shock on page 148 for more information.)

- **Monitor the dog's breathing and heartbeat** and perform rescue breathing/CPR if necessary (see Rescue Breathing and CPR, page 122).

For more information about bloat, see Part 3, page 66.

 ## signs of bloat

- Drooling, retching, or attempting to vomit unsuccessfully
- Pacing, restlessness, or anxious behavior
- Painful, distended abdomen
- Attempting to defecate unsuccessfully
- Signs of shock (see Shock, page 148)

BREEDS AT RISK FOR BLOAT

Any dog can bloat, but certain deep-chested breeds are more at risk, such as:

- Basset hound
- Bloodhound
- Briard
- Doberman pinscher
- German shepherd
- Great Dane
- Greyhound
- Golden retriever
- Gordon setter
- Irish wolfhound
- Irish setter
- Labrador retriever
- Saint Bernard
- Standard poodle
- Weimaraner

Burns

Burns are classified based on depth and severity. First-degree burns are the least serious and involve the superficial layers of the skin. Second-degree burns go deeper, causing the skin to blister and swell. Third-degree burns are the most severe, causing loss of skin and hair, and damage to the blood vessels and deeper tissue. All burns should be treated seriously—even those covering a small area of the body—especially since a dog's fur can often hide the true level of severity. For all but the most minor, superficial burns, seek immediate veterinary treatment.

TREATING HEAT BURNS (I.E., FROM FIRE, STEAM, HOT WATER, OR DIRECT HEAT SOURCES)

- **Immediately flush the burned area with cool water** for 5 to 10 minutes. This will help prevent further damage to deeper tissue by literally reducing the heat level below the surface of the skin. A cool water flush will also provide temporary pain relief. Use a hose, shower, or bucket of water, or even a cool bath if the burn is limited to one area of the body. However, **do not to submerge the dog's entire body in cool water** in severe burn cases—this can cause the dog to go into shock. If multiple body parts are burned, attempt to rinse only the affected areas, or apply cool compresses.

- **Cover the affected area with a sterile, nonstick bandage** or torn, clean bedsheet. Do not use cotton or other material that can stick to the wound. Do not apply any ointments, butter, or creams.

- **Remove the dog's collar if the burn area is near the head or neck.** The residual skin swelling following a burn can make the collar too tight and restrict breathing.

- **Watch for signs of shock** and treat if necessary (see Shock, page 147).

- **Seek immediate veterinary treatment.**

TREATING CHEMICAL BURNS

Chemical burns are caused by caustic substances such as swimming pool treatment products, bleach, toilet bowl cleaners, and weed killers. Exposure happens when these chemicals are accidentally spilled or knocked over onto the dog, or when a dog walks through a liquid on the ground, as with battery acid that's leaked from under a car. Unlike heat burns, chemical burns can continue to burn deeper into the skin long after initial contact, especially since a dog's fur can trap the chemical. The other important difference with chemical burns is that you must protect yourself before treating the dog, or you could be hurt, too.

- **Put on rubber gloves, face mask, eye protection, and any protective clothing** you have available *before* you approach the dog.

- **Remove the dog's collar** if it is anywhere near the burned or contaminated area.

- **Restrain the dog if necessary,** and use a muzzle if he attempts to lick off the chemical.

- **For liquid chemical burns, flush with cool water for at least 20 minutes,** making sure the runoff flows away from the dog's body. If the substance is oily, use a mild grease-cutting dish soap. **For powdered chemical burns,** attempt to brush off as much of the powder as you can before beginning the cool water rinse. Do not apply any ointments, butter, or creams.

- **Watch for signs of shock** and treat if necessary (see Shock, page 147).

- **Seek immediate veterinary treatment.**

Choking

If the dog can breathe and is attempting to cough the object up, let him try without interfering:

- **Watch the dog closely**, giving him a minute or two to cough up the object himself. If he is unsuccessful but still able to breathe without gasping or wheezing, rush him to the vet immediately. Take someone with you if possible to monitor the dog's breathing and react if the situation worsens.

If the dog is struggling, wheezing, gasping, or unable to breathe:

- **Open the mouth and look/feel inside for the stuck object.** Pull the tongue forward toward the front teeth (you might need to use a dish towel or cloth to get a good grip).
- **If you can reach the object, pull it out carefully.** If there is any residual foreign matter or vomit present, use your finger to sweep it away and clear the mouth as much as possible. **DO NOT do a "blind finger sweep"** deep into the dog's throat without looking, or you might accidentally push the object further into the throat. If you can see the object but can't reach it, try using tweezers or forceps. If you still can't pull the object out, go to the next step.

signs of choking

Choking is always an emergency—take action immediately!

- Dog is struggling to breathe/stops breathing
- Dog is agitated and panicked
- Dog is pawing at mouth
- Breathing noises are wheezing and strained
- Gum color turns blue or white

- **If the dog is small enough, pick him up by the hind legs** with the head hanging downward to see if gravity will dislodge the object. **For large dogs, lift the hind legs up like a wheelbarrow,** leaving the front feet on the ground.
- **Perform the canine Heimlich maneuver.** For medium to large dogs: Stand behind the dog and put your arms around his waist. Make a fist with your hand, clasp your other hand over it, and place them in the soft spot just under the bottom of the ribcage. Quickly thrust inward and upward 3 to 5 times, then check to see if the object has dislodged.
- **Give rescue breaths.** If the object still has not dislodged and the dog is unable to breathe, give 5 rescue breaths to try to force some air into the lungs (see Rescue Breathing and CPR, page 122, for instructions).

Back blows

Use the heel of your hand to deliver 1 or 2 sharp blows between the dog's shoulder blades

- **Try back blows.** If these attempts are still unsuccessful, try alternating back blows with the Heimlich maneuver. Continue doing as much as you can while someone drives you and your dog to the vet.
- **Even if the object dislodges, check his breathing** and perform rescue breaths/CPR if necessary as you make your way to the vet (see Rescue Breathing and CPR, page 122).
- **See a vet,** even if the item dislodges, for all but the most minor incidences of choking. There could be damage to the throat, mouth, or esophagus, or respiratory damage requiring treatment.

Drowning

Contrary to popular belief, not all dogs are natural swimmers. But even water-savvy canines can suffer near-drowning accidents by falling into a swimming pool and being unable to locate the steps, becoming trapped under a pool cover, getting caught in strong ocean current, or falling through thin ice.

After any near-drowning rescue, take the dog for immediate veterinary treatment, even if you are able to easily revive him. Serious, delayed breathing problems, as well as the effects of hypothermia, can result anywhere from a few hours to a day after such an accident. The dog may also develop pneumonia.

Never put your life at risk by going into unsafe water to rescue a dog. If you drown too, you'll be no help to anyone. Call for help and proceed with extreme caution.

- **Get the dog onto dry ground.** Use the pole end of a pool net, broomstick, or fishing pole to hook onto the dog's collar and pull him to you. If the dog is far out into open water, use a boogie board or flotation device to help bring him in safely.
- **Drain the lungs of water.** If the dog is small enough, lift him up by the hind legs with the head hanging down for 10 to 20 seconds and give him a few shakes. If the dog is too large to lift, grab the hind legs and raise them up like a wheelbarrow. Your goal is for water to drain out of the mouth. If this doesn't happen quickly and you have someone to help you, have the person thump on the dog's chest briefly to attempt to restart breathing. If this doesn't work after a few seconds, go to the next step.
- **Lay the dog on his side,** placing the lower body on a folded blanket or towel so that the head position is slightly lowered.
- **Give 2 abdominal thrusts.** Place the heel of your hand in the soft indentation just below the center of the ribcage and give 2 thrusts inward and upward toward the dog's head. If water doesn't drain out after a few seconds, go to the next step.
- **Begin rescue breathing** (see Rescue Breathing and CPR, page 122). Give the dog 2 to 4 breaths, watching for the chest to rise. Check for a pulse/heartbeat, and begin CPR if none is present. If a pulse/heartbeat is detectable, continue rescue breathing, giving 15 to 20 breaths per minute until you reach the veterinarian, or until the dog revives.
- **Wrap the dog in a blanket and get immediate veterinary treatment.** Turn the heat on in the car to keep him warm. Watch for signs of shock (see Shock, page 147).

Electric Cord Shock

Electric cord shock happens when a puppy or dog chews on a live electric cord. The resulting injuries can be mild (burns to the lips, tongue, and mouth) to life threatening (circulatory distress, seizures, lung damage, collapse, death).

- **Before you do anything else, disconnect the power.** If the dog is still in contact with the live cord do not touch him until the power is shut off or you could be electrocuted, too. Throw the main circuit breaker or, wearing rubber gloves, unplug the cord. If you can't do either quickly, look for a nonconductive item like a wooden chair or broomstick to move the dog away from the cord. Keep yourself and the dog away from wet surfaces, which conduct electricity.
- **Perform CPR if needed.** If the dog has collapsed, check his breathing and for a heartbeat or pulse and begin rescue breathing and/or CPR if necessary (see Rescue Breathing and CPR, page 122).
- **If the dog is conscious, check for mouth burns.** Flush mouth burns with cool water, or apply an ice pack to burns on the lips while you take him to the vet.
- **Keep the dog calm.** Speak softly, stay calm, and provide a quiet environment as you proceed to the vet. The dog will likely be upset, and if he's suffered any lung or circulatory damage, you will want to do all you can to keep him breathing normally.
- **Watch for signs of shock** and treat if necessary (see Shock, page 147).
- **Get immediate veterinary treatment,** even if there is no evidence of injury. In some cases, signs may not be visible for days after the incident.

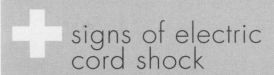

signs of electric cord shock

- Dog cries out in pain with cord in his mouth, unable to let go of cord
- Burn marks on mouth, tongue, or lips
- Burning odor
- Bite marks visible on electric cords
- Difficulty breathing
- Seizures
- Dog is collapsed near electric cord

SEIZURES RESULTING FROM ELECTRIC SHOCK

Sometimes electric cord shock can cause seizures. Although they can be frightening to witness, it is likely the seizure will end within a few seconds or minutes. Keep the dog safe by removing any obstacles nearby and turn down the lights or place a towel loosely over his eyes to create a dark environment. Do not shake the dog or try to speak to him. Proceed to the vet as soon as the seizure has ended.

Fractures and Limb Injuries

Fractures and other limb injuries are not life threatening in and of themselves—however, the pain, trauma, and blood loss that often result can quickly cause a dog to go into shock or respiratory distress, which is an emergency. Since many fractures are caused by falls or car accidents, there could also be internal injuries present. For these reasons, any fracture should be treated as a serious injury requiring fast veterinary treatment.

If a dog has fractured his back or pelvis, follow the instructions for transporting a critically injured dog on page 129.

- **Check for signs of shock or respiratory distress.** Watch the dog closely as you proceed to treat the fracture (see Rescue Breathing and CPR, page 122, and Shock, page 147) and take immediate action if necessary. If there are no signs of these, move on to the next step.
- **Keep the dog quiet and calm, and muzzle/restrain him if possible.** Fractures are extremely painful, which can cause even the gentlest dog to bite.
- **If the bone is protruding outside the skin, don't move it.** Leave the bone in the position you found it.
- **Wash the area of exposed bone with saline** (such as contact lens solution, or 1 teaspoon (6 g) salt added to a quart [946 ml] of warm water) and cover with a sterile, nonstick pad, dressing, or clean cloth. Secure the dressing with tape a few inches (7.5 cm) beyond the exposed bone, taking care not to disturb the bone or wrap the dressing too tightly. Exposed bone is highly prone to infection, so be sure to keep the dressing clean.

- **Determine whether or not to splint.** If you are less than thirty minutes from the vet, forgo making a splint unless you're unable to keep the dog still and you think he'll further injure himself. A pet carrier or kennel can help immobilize the dog as you drive. If you're unable keep the dog still and feel a splint is necessary, go to the next step.
- **Splint the limb in the position you found it.** Begin by wrapping the injured limb comfortably in a soft towel or cloth. Next, find something rigid (a rolled-up magazine, newspaper, or sticks for a large dog; pens, pencils, or tongue depressors for a small dog) and place it around or on either side of the limb to provide stability. Secure the splint at multiple sites above and below the fracture with tape, cloth strips, plastic wrap, or panty hose. Be careful not to disturb the position of the injured limb. Do not wrap the splint too tightly—you should be able to slip a finger between the limb and the material you've tied it with.
- **Get immediate veterinary treatment.**

Making a splint can be challenging, and doing it wrong can cause more harm than good. Do not splint the limb if you don't have the tools to do it correctly.

 ## signs of a fracture

- Pain
- Swelling
- Bone protruding from skin
- Lameness
- Abnormal limb position

Splinting Injured Limbs

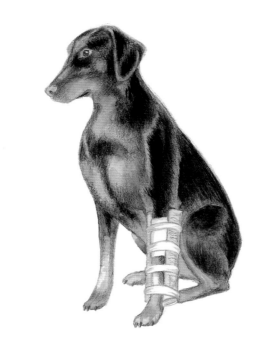

Make sure the splinting material reaches all the way up the leg. A rolled-up newspaper or magazine works well, since it can be easily wrapped around the limb and tied with cloth strips, torn sheeting, or panty hose.

If you have no rigid surface to make a splint, you can use the dog's opposite uninjured leg. Place a soft cloth in between the two limbs and tie the two legs together. Don't tie them too tight—you should be able to slip your finger in between the wrapping and the limb.

Heatstroke (Hyperthermia)

Heatstroke happens when a dog gets severely over-heated, usually with a body temperature above 104°F (40°C). Normal temperature range is 100.2°F to 102.8°F (37.9°C to 39.3°C). Any dog can get heatstroke, but certain dogs are more at risk: short-nosed breeds like boxers, pugs, and bulldogs; dogs that are overweight; dogs with heart or lung conditions; elderly dogs; and those that are out of shape physically.

Heatstroke can kill dogs very quickly. **Your first priority is to cool them safely.**

- **Rush the dog to a cool, well-ventilated area.** Lay the dog on a cool floor. Have someone get a fan and turn it on near the dog if possible.
- **Take the dog's temperature.** (see Temperature, page 15). If there is someone to help you, have them prepare to cool the dog by getting a garden hose or filling a bucket of cool water and getting towels and ice packs ready. If possible, have them place a cool, wet towel on the dog's head and neck while you take the dog's temperature.
- If the dog is unconscious or the body temperature is above 106°F (41°C), proceed immediately to the vet if you're less than five minutes away. Turn the air-conditioning on high as you drive. If you have someone to help you, bring an ice pack or bag of frozen peas, some towels, and a bucket of cool water. **Take special care to cool the head first,** using the frozen pack wrapped in a towel. Place wet towels on the dog's underside, head, neck, and feet.
- If you are more than five minutes from the vet and/or the dog is conscious, begin cooling him as follows: Use a garden hose (make sure the water is coming out cool before you begin) to spray the dog down for several minutes. If there is no access to a garden hose, lay cool, wet towels on the dog's head, neck, chest, stomach, and feet. Give him a bowl of cool water and let him drink as much as he wants. Provide ventilation with an electric fan, if possible. You can also take cotton balls soaked with rubbing alcohol and rub them on his feet, groin, and underarm area (but do this sparingly—using more than a half pint [236 ml] of rubbing alcohol can be toxic).
- **Recheck the dog's temperature every five minutes** to see if it has come down. Continue cooling the dog until his body temperature gets below 106°F (41°C), then keep him cool as you drive to the vet. **Stop cooling the dog when his body temperature reaches 104°F (40°C).**

signs of heatstroke

- Bright red gum color in early stages; pale, blue, or gray in late stages
- Panting heavily, thick saliva
- Body temperature above 104°F (40°C)
- Increased heart rate and respiratory rate
- Disorientation, "drunken" behavior, depression
- Vomiting or diarrhea, with or without the presence of blood
- Capillary refill time is too fast (see Capillary Refill Time, page 15)
- Shock (see Shock, page 147)
- Collapse, coma

- **Check for signs of shock** (see Shock, page 147) and treat if necessary, but do not warm the dog or wrap him in a blanket if his temperature is above 103°F (39°C).
- **Monitor the dog's breathing** and be prepared to perform CPR if necessary.
- **Get immediate veterinary treatment** once the dog's body temperature is safely below 106°F (41°C).

Notes:

Do not submerge the dog in cold or icy water! Over-chilling a dog with heatstroke can be extremely dangerous.

Do not muzzle a dog with heatstroke—this may interfere with his ability to pant heavily and cool himself down.

how to prevent heatstroke

- Never leave your dog in a hot car, even with the windows rolled down. If it's warmer than 70°F (21°C) outside, it is unsafe for a dog—even in the shade or with the windows rolled down. Dogs being left in parked cars is the most common cause of heatstroke.

- Always provide shade, ventilation, and water for dogs left outdoors.

- Do not overexercise a dog in hot, humid weather. Watch the dog for signs of fatigue and heavy panting, and provide plenty of shade and water on outings.

- Take special care with short-nosed breeds like bulldogs, pugs, boxers, and Pekingese or dogs that are old, overweight, out of shape, or have heart or lung conditions.

- Dogs with a previous history of heatstroke are at a higher risk to get it again.

Insect Stings and Snake Bites

Dogs often get stung by bees and wasps, usually resulting only in minor swelling and discomfort that can be treated with simple first aid: scrape the stinger out using the edge of a credit card, then apply a cold compress or baking soda poultice.

However, sometimes dogs can have severe allergic reactions, causing their faces to swell tremendously and requiring a trip to the vet for an injection of anti-histamine and/or steroid to bring the swelling down. These dogs should be watched closely to make sure the swelling doesn't affect their airway function.

The most severe type of reaction to an insect sting is anaphylactic shock. Although rare, you will know immediately when it happens because the dog will experience vomiting, diarrhea, and difficulty breathing, and can collapse and die within minutes. Be prepared to perform CPR as you rush to the nearest emergency hospital.

TREATING ANAPHYLACTIC SHOCK

• **Transport the dog immediately to the nearest veterinary hospital.** If the dog is conscious, grab an anti-histamine on your way out the door and call the vet to see if it should be given. The usual dose is 1 milligram per pound of body weight for diphenhydramine (the active ingredient in such brands as Benadryl). Other antihistamines may have different dosing guidelines.
• **Check for signs of shock.** If signs are present (pale gums; a weak, rapid pulse; restlessness; rapid breathing; and possibly vomiting or diarrhea), wrap the dog in a blanket as you transport him to the hospital (see Shock, page 147, for more information).
• **Be prepared to give rescue breathing/CPR.** Bring someone with you if possible and monitor the dog's breathing and perform rescue breathing/CPR if necessary (see Rescue Breathing and CPR, page 122).

TREATING HEAD SWELLING/SEVERE ALLERGIC REACTIONS

If the dog's face, muzzle, and ears begin to swell but he does not show signs of shock or respiratory distress, call the vet for instructions on whether to give an antihistamine at home first, or drive straight over for an injection and further treatment (or both). After treatment, you will likely have to continue watching the dog closely for the next twelve hours and give a course of oral antihistamines.

To remove a stinger, use a credit card, butter knife, or cardboard to scrape it out using a flicking motion. Do not use tweezers or try to squeeze or pick out the stinger.

signs of a snakebite

• Bite marks on the dog's skin, usually on the head, face, or neck area
• Swelling, bleeding, and redness at the bitten area
• Pain
• Trembling, twitching, or drooling
• Difficulty breathing or respiratory arrest
• Signs of shock (see Shock, page 147)

TYPES OF POISONOUS SNAKES

Copperhead: The top of the triangular head is a copper/orange color. Average length is 2 to 4 feet (0.6 to 1.2 m). Body has hourglass-shaped markings. No rattle.

Coral Snake: Small head, no discernible neck. The body has red stripes next to yellow stripes next to black stripes. Average length is 3 feet (1 m).

Rattlesnake: Head is triangular with a discernible neck. The tail has a rattle. Length up to 8 feet (2.5 m).

Water Moccasin or Cottonmouth: These snakes reside in swampy areas and streams. They average 5 feet (1.5 m) in length with a dark-colored body, triangular head, and white color inside the mouth.

When seeking treatment for snakebite, always call the vet prior to your arrival to make sure they have the antivenin. If they don't, they may send you to another animal hospital instead.

TREATING SNAKEBITES

Snakebites tend to happen on the face and neck area of curious dogs. Since it's hard to tell the difference between a harmless and a deadly snake, all bites should be treated as an emergency—especially if you're in an area where venomous snakes are known to reside. If you can safely attempt to identify the snake by noting its head shape and body markings, do so. If you must kill the snake to protect yourself or the dog, do not reach down to pick it up—a decapitated snake remains venomous and can still reflexively "bite" up to an hour after being killed. If you can use a long tool to carefully slide the dead snake into a bag, take it with you to the vet for identification—but only if you can do this within a minute or two.

- **Remove the dog's collar.** Swelling in the head and neck area can make the collar tighten and constrict the dog's airway.
- **Check for signs of breathing difficulty or respiratory arrest.** Poisonous bites can cause the airway to swell shut or paralyze the respiratory system. Be prepared to begin rescue breathing/CPR if needed (see Rescue Breathing and CPR, page 122).
- **Watch for signs of shock** (see Shock, page 147) and treat if necessary.
- **Rinse the bite area with water** to help flush away residual venom. **Do not cut or suck on the wound!**
- **Keep the dog calm and immobile.** Movement can cause the toxin to circulate through the bloodstream faster. Carry the dog to the car if you can, or transport him using a sheet or towel as a stretcher (you'll need someone to hold the other end). If you can't do either, have the dog walk slowly to the car. Once inside, keep the bite area lower than the heart if possible.
- **Transport the dog immediately to the nearest veterinary hospital.** If possible, call ahead to make sure they have a supply of antivenin. If not, they may send you to another hospital that does.

Poisoning

Dogs most often become poisoned by eating something they shouldn't, but poisons can also be inhaled or absorbed through the skin.

The symptoms of poisoning vary widely depending on the type of poison, and can develop immediately or not until days later. **All poisonings are an emergency. Take immediate action the moment you discover a potential poisoning or notice the following signs in the dog:**

- Severe vomiting or diarrhea (with or without blood)
- Seizures, trembling, twitching, or extreme anxious behavior
- Red, blue, gray, or pale gum color (normal color is pink)
- Depression, drowsiness, "drunken" behavior, uncoordination
- Heavy drooling or foaming at the mouth
- Swollen, irritated, watering eyes or red, inflamed skin
- Burns on the lips, tongue, or mouth
- Bleeding from the mouth, nose, ears, or anus
- Coughing heavily, difficulty breathing, collapse

For all types of poisoning, take a brief moment to identify the type and amount of poison involved, and when the exposure took place. If possible, take the package or bottle containing the poison and a sample of any vomit/stool sealed in a plastic bag with you to the hospital—this will help them identify the proper antidote.

TREATING INGESTED POISONS

- **Check for signs of stopped breathing or stopped heart** and give rescue breathing/CPR if necessary (see Rescue Breathing and CPR, page 122).
- **Call the poison control hotline or your veterinarian.** Be ready to give the dog's age, breed, and weight; the type and quantity of poison involved; and when the incident happened.
- **Make the dog vomit.** If the poison was swallowed and is **not** caustic, you will likely be instructed to make the dog vomit immediately. To do this you'll need a measuring spoon, 3 percent hydrogen peroxide, and either an oral syringe/eyedropper or a saucer of milk. Give the dog 1 tablespoon (15 ml) per 20 pounds (9 kg) body weight of hydrogen peroxide orally. For dogs under 20 pounds (9 kg), give 1 to 2 teaspoons (5 to 10 ml) per 10 pounds (5 kg) body weight. Mix it with a little milk in a saucer to see if he'll drink it willingly. If not, you'll have to use the oral syringe/eyedropper and squirt it down his throat. The dog should vomit within a few minutes. If not, the dose can be repeated up to 3 times, 15 minutes apart.
- **Ask about activated charcoal.** If you have activated charcoal in your dog's first-aid kit, tell the vet or poison hotline. Depending on how long it's been since the poison was ingested and how far away you are from the hospital, they may instruct you on how to use it.
- **Go immediately to the nearest veterinary hospital.** If you've only been speaking to the poison center, be sure to call the vet and let them know you're on your way. Many times the poison hotline will also call the vet to consult with them on the best treatment.

When not to induce vomiting. Never induce vomiting if a dog is unconscious, depressed, woozy, or is having seizures or difficulty breathing. Under these conditions, the dog could suffocate on his vomit. Never induce vomiting if the swallowed poison is caustic (such as bleach, acids, and petroleum-based products)—this will burn the dog's throat and cause even more damage on its way up. If you have the product's package, check the label for instructions on what to do if accidentally swallowed.

TREATING TOPICAL POISONS

If the dog has had a toxic substance such as motor oil, paint, turpentine, or insecticide spilled on his coat or skin, your first step is to wash it off as quickly as possible to stop the absorption.

- **For non-oily substances,** flush the area with water for several minutes.
- **For oil-based substances**, use a mild, grease-cutting dishwashing liquid and water.
- **To treat the eye area**, use water or a sterile eye wash.
- **If the poison is in powder form**, dust, brush, or vacuum as much off as possible before washing with plenty of water and shampoo or mild dishwashing liquid.
- **Call your veterinarian or poison hotline** to see if further treatment is recommended.

When treating tropical poisons, wear rubber gloves to protect yourself.

The ASPCA's Animal Poison Control Center hotline is 888.426.4435. Serving all of North America, they have veterinarians on call 24 hours a day, 7 days a week. A consultation fee may be charged to your credit card after they've helped you. **If you live outside North America,** call your veterinarian or local human poison control center (which usually has pet poison information) in a poisoning emergency.

Signs of toxic inhalation include coughing, choking, cherry red gums, twitching, trembling, seizures, respiratory problems, and unconsciousness.

TREATING INHALED POISONS

Inhaled poisons include carbon monoxide from leaks in gas and propane home heaters; smoke inhalation from being trapped in a fire; ammonia gas from harsh cleansers; chemical fumes from weed killers and pesticides; and fumes from oil-based paints. Dogs are most often exposed to inhaled poisons when they're confined in an unventilated area.

- **Get the dog to fresh air immediately.**
- **Check for stopped breathing/stopped heart** and administer rescue breathing/CPR if necessary (see Rescue Breathing and CPR, page 122).
- **Check the dog's gum color and capillary refill time** (see Capillary Refill Time, page 15). A dog's normal gum color is pink. Bright red and other gum colors like blue or gray will help the vet determine the dog's state.
- **Watch for shock** and treat if necessary (see Shock, page 147).
- **Call the vet** for specific instructions and transport to the animal hospital.
- **Poisoning can sometimes cause seizures.** If this happens, it is likely the seizure will end within a couple of minutes. Keep the dog safe by removing any obstacles nearby and turn down the lights or place a towel loosely over his eyes to create a dark environment. Do not try to hold his tongue or put your hands in his mouth. Do not shake the dog or try to speak to him during or immediately after the seizure. When it has ended, wrap the dog in a towel or blanket and transport to the vet.

Shock

Shock is a life-threatening condition that occurs when there is a drop in blood flow and oxygen to the internal organs. Many types of serious injury or illness can lead to shock, including blood loss, severe trauma (such as from a car accident), severe allergic reactions (anaphylactic shock), and blood infections (septic shock). **Immediate first aid and veterinary treatment are essential for all cases of shock.** If left untreated, a dog can quickly go into cardiac arrest.

TREATING SHOCK

- **If the dog is unconscious,** check for breathing and heartbeat/pulse and administer rescue breathing/CPR if necessary.
- **Control bleeding.** If shock is resulting from blood loss, control the bleeding quickly to prevent a further drop in blood flow/oxygen to the body (see Bleeding, page 130).
- **Stabilize the dog if necessary.** If there are broken bones or a spinal injury, stabilize the dog for transport to the vet (see Safe Transportation to the Vet, page 128). **Cover the dog with a blanket, coat, or towel** to keep them warm.
- **Elevate the hind end slightly** by placing a folded towel under the dog's hindquarters (do not do this if you suspect a spinal/back injury or if it causes pain).
- **Get immediate veterinary treatment.** If you have someone with you, have the person very gently massage the dog's legs and muscles (if there are no broken bones) to help maintain blood circulation as you drive to the veterinary hospital.

SIGNS OF SHOCK

Early Shock

- Increased heart rate and pulse
- Reddish gum color
- Capillary refill time of 1 to 2 seconds
- "Pounding" pulse

Middle Stages

- Low body temperature
- Cool limbs and pads
- Weak, rapid pulse
- Pale gums/mucous membranes
- Slow capillary refill time (over 3 seconds)
- Woozy, weakened mental state

Late Stages

- Slow respiratory and heart rate
- Weak or no pulse
- Depressed mental state, unconsciousness
- Stopped breathing, cardiac arrest

CONCLUSION

In writing *The Safe Dog Handbook,* my goal was to create a complete reference guide to help you keep your dog safe indoors and out, from puppyhood through the golden years. To accomplish this goal, a full array of canine hazards was explored in great detail. The irony here is that just reading about these dangers is enough to make even the most sensible dog owner a bit anxious—much like a new parent might feel after reading a book about baby proofing.

Now is a good time for a little perspective. Of the millions of pet dogs out there, the likelihood that something bad will happen to yours is actually quite small. And now that you've read this book, your dog has an even better chance of staying safe because you know how to spot hazards, prevent accidents, and respond to emergencies.

That said, it's also important to remember that no matter how well prepared we are, sometimes accidents happen anyway. It's no one's fault—just simple bad luck. The best we can do is take precautions when appropriate, and not become bogged down with worry.

So revel in each slobbery kiss, each satisfying game of fetch, each heart-melting puppy snore—that's what living with dogs is all about, right?

I hope you've enjoyed learning all about canine safety, and that this book will help bring you greater confidence and enjoyment as you and your dog go about your daily adventures. Have fun out there … and remember to buckle up the pooch!

TOXIC PLANT GUIDE

This list contains plants that have been reported as having systemic effects on animals and/or intense effects on the gastrointestinal tract.

Please note that the information contained in this list is not meant to be all inclusive, but rather a compilation of the most frequently encountered plants. If you think that your dog may have ingested a poisonous substance, contact your local veterinarian or 24-hour emergency poison hotline immediately.

ASPCA Animal Poison Control Center
888.426.4435 (North America; fees apply)

Vetfone 24-Hour Helpline:
09065 00 55 00 (UK; fees apply)

COMMON NAME	SCIENTIFIC NAME
a	
Aloe	*Aloe vera*
Amaryllis	*Amaryllis* sp
Andromeda Japonica	*Pieris japonica*
Asian Lily (Liliaceae)	*Lilium asiatica*
Asparagus Fern	*Asparagus sprenger*
Australian Nut	*Macadamia integrifolia*
Autumn Crocus	*Colchicum autumnale*
Avocado	*Persea Americana*
Azalea	*Rhododendron* spp
b	
Bird of Paradise	*Caesalpinia gilliesii*
American Bittersweet	*Celastrus scandens*
European Bittersweet	*Solanum dulcamara*
Branching Ivy	*Hedera helix*
Buckeye	*Aesculus* spp
Buddist Pine	*Podocarpus macrophylla*

TOXIC PLANT GUIDE

C

Caladium .... *Caladium hortulanum*

Calla Lily .... *Zantedeschia aethiopiea*

Castor Bean.. *Ricinus communis*

Ceriman (aka Cutleaf........................... *Monstera deliciosa*
Philodendron)

Charming Dieffenbachia .... *Dieffenbachia amoena*

Chinaberry Tree .... *Melia azedarach*

Chinese Evergreen .... *Aglaonema modestrum*

Christmas Rose .... *Helleborus niger*

Clematis .... *Clematis* sp

Cordatum .... *Philodendron oxycardium*

Corn Plant .... *Dracaena* spp
(aka Cornstalk Plant)

Cutleaf Philodendron .... *Monstera deliciosa*
(aka Ceriman)

Cycads .... *Cycas and Zamia* sp

Cyclamen .... *Cyclamen* spp

d

Daffodil .... *Narcissus* spp

Day Lily .... *Hemerocallis* spp

Deadly Nightshade .... *Solanum* spp
(*see* Nightshade)

Devil's Ivy .... *Epipremnum aureum*

Dumb Cane .... *Dieffenbachia*

e

f

g

TOXIC PLANT GUIDE

h

Hahn's self branching English Ivy ...... *Hedera helix*
Heartleaf Philodendron .... *Philodendron oxycardium*
Heavenly Bamboo .... *Nandina domestica*
Holly .... *Ilex* spp
Hops .... *Humulus lupulus*
Horsehead Philodendron .... *Philodendron bipennifolium*
Hurricane Plant .... *Monstera deliciosa*
Hyacinth .... *Hyacinthus oreintalis*
Hydrangea .... *Hydrangea macrophylla*

i

Iris .... *Iris* sp

j

Japanese Show Lily .... *Lilium* sp
Japanese Yew (aka Yew) .... *Taxus* sp
Jerusalem Cherry .... *Solanum pseudocapsicum*

k

Kalanchoe .... *Kalanchoe* spp

l

Lace Fern .... *Asparagus setaceus*
Lacy Tree .... *Philodendron selloum*
Lily of the Valley .... *Convalaria majalis*

m

Macadamia Nut .... *Macadamia integrifolia*

Madagascar Dragon Tree .... *Dracaena marginata*

Marble Queen.................................... *Scindapsus aureus*

Marijuana.. *Cannabis sativa*

Mauna Loa Peace Lily .... *Spathiphyllum*
(aka Peace Lily)

Mexican Breadfruit .... *Onstera deliciosa*

Mistletoe "American" .... *Phoradendron* spp

Morning Glory.................................... *Ipomoea* spp

Mother-in-Law................................... *Monstera deliciosa*

n

Narcissus... *Narcissus* spp

Needlepoint Ivy .... *Hedera helix*

Nephthytis... *Syngonium podopyllum*

Nightshade.. *Solanum* spp

o

Oleander .... *Nerium oleander*

Onion... *Allium* spp

Orange Day Lily .... *Hemorocallis graminea*

TOXIC PLANT GUIDE

p

Panda	*Philodendron panduraeformae*
Peace Lily (aka Mauna Loa Peace Lily)	*Spathiphyllum*
Philodendron Pertusum	*Philodendron spp*
Plumosa Fern	*Asparagus plumosus*
Precatory Bean	*Abrus precatorius*

q

Queensland Nut	*Macadamia integrifolia*

r

Red Emerald	*Philodendron*
Red Lily	*Lilium umbellatum*
Red-Margined Dracaena (aka Straight-Margined Dracaena)	*Dracaena marginata*
Red Princess	*Philodendron*
Rhododendron	*Rhododendron spp*
Ribbon Plant	*Dracaena sanderiana*
Rubrum Lily	*Lilium* spp

s

Saddle Leaf Philodendron	*Philodendron selloum*
Sago Palm	*Cycas* and *Zamia* sp
Satin Pothos	*Scindapsus* spp
Schefflera	*Schefflera* or *Brassaia actinophylla*
Spotted Dumb Cane	*Dieffenbachia picta*

Stargazer Lily .... *Lilium orientalis*
Striped Dracaena .... *Dracaena deremensis*
Sweetheart Ivy .... *Hedera helix*
Swiss Cheese Plant .... *Monstera deliciosa*

†

Taro Vine.. *Scindapsus aureus*
Tiger Lily... *Lilium tigrinum*
Tomato Plant .... *Lycopersicon* spp
Tree Philodendron .... *Philodendron bipinnatifidum*
Tropic Snow Dumbcane .... *Dieffenbachia amoena*
Tulip .... *Tulip* sp

V

Variable Dieffenbachia .... *Dieffenbachia picta*
Variegated Philodendron .... *Scindapsus Philodendron* spp

W

Warneckei Dracaena .... *Dracaena dermensis*
Wood Lily .... *Lilium umbellatum*

Y

Yesterday, Today, Tomorrow.............. *Brunfelsia australis*
Yew (aka Japanese Yew) .... *Taxus* sp
Yucca... *Yucca* sp

Copyright © 2008. The American Society for the Prevention of Cruelty to Animals (ASPCA). All Rights Reserved.

appendix ii

FOOD GUIDE

A quick reference to some foods that can be toxic to dogs, as well as some safe alternatives.

Foods That Can Be Toxic to Dogs

Alcoholic drinks

Avocado

Bread dough and items containing uncooked yeast

Chocolate (dark and baker's chocolate are worse than milk chocolate)

Coffee/coffee grounds

Fruit seeds and pits (pips), moderate to large quantities

Garlic, large quantities

Grapes

High-fat foods like turkey skin, bacon fat, gravy, etc.

Hops (typically found in home brewing kits)

Macadamia nuts

Moldy food/trash

Onions, chives, and onion powder

Raisins (sultanas)

Salt, large quantities

Spices such as nutmeg, paprika, and turmeric (large quantities)

Tea and tea bags (caffeinated)

Xylitol (a common sugar substitute)

Safe Food Treats

The following foods are all considered safe for dogs when fed as treats or snacks in reasonable quantities, although dogs with sensitive stomachs may experience mild digestive upset with any new food.

Apple slices

Banana

Blueberries

Canned plain pumpkin or cooked butternut squash

Carrots, steamed or raw, cut into bite-size pieces

Cooked chicken, turkey, salmon, liver, or other meat (avoid skin, fat, and seasonings)

Egg, hard boiled

Green beans, steamed

Peanut butter (in modest quantities)

Sardines (bones and skin are fine here)

Sweet potato, baked

Yogurt, plain

First Aid Supplies and Instruction

First-Aid Guide Books

Be Red Cross Ready Safety Series Vol. 2: *Dog First Aid.* StayWell Publishing, 2007 www.redcrossstore.org

Pet First Aid and Disaster Response Guide by G. Elaine Acker. Pets America Publications, 2007— www.barnesandnoble.com

First-Aid Instruction

Petco—www.petco.com (online)

Pet Tech—www.pettech.net (hands-on)

Red Cross—www.redcross.org (hands-on)

Pet Emergency First Aid: Dogs. *Apogee Communications Group* www.amazon.com (DVD)

First-Aid Kits

Orvis—www.orvis.com

Pets Ready—www.petsready.com

Red Cross—www.redcrossshop.org/firstaid

Riley Care—www.rileycare.com

Muzzles

Drs. Foster and Smith www.drsfostersmith.com

PetSmart—www.petsmart.com

Oral Syringes

Drs. Foster and Smith www.drsfostersmith.com

Revival Animal Health www.revivalanimal.com

Miscellaneous Safety Products

Riley Care—www.rileycare.com

Toxiban Activated Charcoal

Jeffers—www.jefferspet.com

Revival Animal Health www.revivalanimal.com

Pet-Safe Home and Garden Products

"Doggie Damage Control" Products

Door Shield—www.improvementscatalog.com

Nature's Miracle Enzyme Stain and Odor Remover—www.naturemakesitwork.com

Scat Mat Electronic Training Mat www.drsfostersmith.com

Fertilizer, Weed Killers, and Other Garden Products

Garden Safe—www.gardensafe.com

Pet-Friendly Fertilizer—www.petfriendly.com

WOW!® Plus Pre-Emergence Weed Control and Fertilizer—www.gardensalive.com

RESOURCES

Home Care

Method—www.methodhome.com

PetGanics—www.petganics.com

Seventh Generation
www.seventhgeneration.com

Simple Green—www.simplegreen.com

Ice-Melting Product

Safe Paw Ice Melter—www.safepaw.com

Pet-Safe Slug and Snail Bait

Garden Safe—www.gardensafe.com

Sluggo—www.montereylawngarden.com

Books on Natural Cleaning

Baking Soda: Over 500 Fabulous, Fun and Frugal Uses You've Probably Never Thought Of by Vicki Lansky. Book Peddlers, 2003 www.amazon.com

Green Clean: The Environmentally Sound Guide to Cleaning Your Home by Linda Mason Hunter and Mikki Halpin. Melcher Media, 2005— www.amazon.com

Pet Insurance

ASPCA Pet Insurance
www.aspcapetinsurance.com

Pets Best Insurance—www.petsbest.com

Veterinary Pet Insurance
www.petinsurance.com

Microchipping and Tattoo Companies

AKC Companion Animal Recovery (microchips and tattoos)—www.akccar.org

Home Again Companion Animal Retrieval Microchip System—www.homeagain.com

National Dog Registry (tattoos only) www.nationaldogregistry.com

Pool and Boating Safety Products

Doggie Boat Ladder by Paws Aboard www.pawsaboard.com

Ruffwear K-9 Float Coat www.ruffwear.com

Safety Turtle Pool Alarm www.safetyturtle.com

Car Safety Products

Orvis—www.orvis.com

Outward Hound by Kyjen—www.kyjen.com

Petco—www.petco.com

Dog Toys

Busy Buddy brand toys including Tug-a-Jug, Twist n' Treat, and Bouncy Bone, manufactured by Premier Pet products www.premier.com

Kong brand toys, including classic Kong and Kong Time Dispenser www.kongcompany.com

Plush Puppies brand toys including IQube, Intellibone, Pull-A Parts, and Puzzle-Plush Animal Puzzles, manufactured by Kyjen www.kyjen.com

Diet and Nutrition

Companion Animal Sciences Institute (CASI) online canine nutrition courses www.casinstitute.com

Home-Prepared Dog & Cat Diets by Donald Strombeck, DVM. Wiley-Blackwell, 1999 www.amazon.com (book by leading veterinary nutritionist offering sample diets for healthy dogs and dogs with specific medical conditions)

Nutrition consulting services by Catherine Lane, Dip. CFN—www.thepossiblecanine.com

Nutrition consulting services by PetDiets www.petdiets.com

Training Books and DVDs

101 Dog Tricks by Kyra Sundance and Chalcy. Quarry Books; 2007—www.amazon.com

"Lassie, Come!" by Patricia McConnell (DVD)— www.dogwise.com (excellent, effective training advice to teach your dog to come when called)

Take A Bow … Wow! Fun and Functional Dog Tricks by Virginia Broitman and Sherri Lippman. Video PAL-European—www.dogwise.com

Camping, Hiking and Snow Gear

Musher's Secret Paw Balm www.jefferspet.com

Outward Hound by Kyjen—www.kyjen.com

Ruffwear—www.ruffwear.com

Emergency Preparedness

Emergency Preparedness Products
Riley Care—www.rileycare.com

Evacuation Harness
Rock-n-Rescue dog harness— www.rocknrescue.com/acatalog/ Dog-Harness.html

RESOURCES

"Pets Inside" Window Decals
Drs. Foster and Smith
www.drsfostersmith.com

Riley Care—www.rileycare.com

"Red Flag" Fire Warning Updates
National Weather Service (U.S.)
http://fire.boi.noaa.gov

Poison Hotlines and Information

24-Hour Hotlines
ASPCA Animal Poison Center Hotline
(North America) 1.888.426.4435 (fees apply)

Vetfone 24-hour Helpline (U.K.)
09065 00 55 00 (fees apply)

Pet Poison Helpline (U.S. and Canada)
1.800.213.6680 (fees apply)

Pesticide Information
National Pesticide Information Center (U.S.)
1.800.858.7378

Poison Information
ASPCA—www.aspca.org

Natural Anxiety Remedies

Rescue Remedy—www.rescueremedy.com

Ultra Calm dog biscuits
www.drsfostersmith.com

Break-Away Collars

KeepSafe Collar by Premier
www.premier.com

Animal Welfare Organizations

American Society for the Prevention of
Cruelty to Animals—www.aspca.org

Humane Society of the United States
www.hsus.org

Much Love Animal Rescue
www.muchlove.org

PetSmart Charities
www.petsmartcharities.org

Royal Society for the Prevention of
Cruelty to Animals—www.rspca.org.uk

Assistance Dog Programs

Canine Companions for Independence
www.cci.org (provides highly trained
assistance dogs to people with disabilities)

Pet Sitting Organizations

Pet Sitters International
www.petsit.com

National Association of Professional
Pet Sitters
www.petsitters.org

UK Petsitters
www.ukpetsitters.com

All Canadian Pet Services Network
www.acpsn.com

INDEX

INDEX

INDEX

PHOTOGRAPHER CREDITS

Mary Aarons, 20; 100; 111

Andrea Abramovich, 7 (bottom); 31; 74; 88; 99; 117

Chris Amaral/www.gettyimages.com, 2; 52

Nola Anderson, 37

Steven Beaver, 86; 115

Kristin Ellison, 89

John Foxx/www.gettyimages.com, 54

Linda Fund, 101 (top)

GK Hart/Vikki Hart/www.gettyimages.com, 75

Noel Hendrickson/www.gettyimages.com, 72; 106

Wilfried Krecichwost/www.gettyimages.com, 103

William Kiester, 101 (bottom)

Jayne Levant, 93

Ofer Lichtman, 6 (bottom); 66

William Mackenzie-Smith, 22

Chris Mancinelli, 59

Ryan McVay/www.gettyimages.com, 70

Mark Monteiro, 5; 7 (top); 8; 87; 105

Lee Moreno-Lesser, 10

Patricia Mack Newton, 6 (top); 19

Courtesy of Orvis/www.orvis.com, 12; 23; 41; 104

Purestock/www.gettyimages.com, 79

Nick Ridley/www.nickridley.com, 3; 35; 36; 38; 40; 42; 90

Dana Saputo, 50

Steven Schmidt, 98

Dimitri Vervitsiotis/www.gettyimages.com, 76; 168

www.istockphoto.com, 17; 25; 28; 27; 39; 44; 46; 47; 49; 51; 61; 63; 64; 73; 77; 78; 80; 82; 85; 91; 92; 94; 97; 109; 110; 112; 114; 118

www.shutterstock.com, 29; 60; 67

ACKNOWLEDGMENTS

To my wonderful husband, Mark, who said, "You should put all this stuff in a book." Little did he know what he was getting himself into. He remained enthusiastic and uncomplaining throughout, despite being made to eat nothing but frozen food in the final two-month stretch while I continued to cook for the dog. All this, and handsome to boot. After ten years I still feel like I've won the lottery.

A huge thank you to Rochelle Bourgault for her insight in shaping the content, as well as Betsy Gammons, Regina Grenier, Winnie Prentiss, and the talented staff at Quarry. Your enthusiasm and guidance helped turn the intimidating concept of writing a book into a fun and exciting endeavor.

My deepest gratitude to the veterinarians who generously contributed their time and expertise to the project: Richard Palmquist, DVM, chief medical director of the Centinela Animal Hospital in Inglewood, California; Jonnie Quantz, DVM, hospital director of the Animal Emergency Referral Center in Torrance, California; Dean Graulich, DVM, director of the Malibu Coast Animal Hospital in Malibu, California; Amy Brown, DVM, of the Animal Emergency Referral Center in Torrance, California; and to the ASPCA for their kind permission in sharing their toxic plant information.

To the awesome behaviorists, trainers and canine professionals for their invaluable advice: Brian Lee of Way of the Dog Canine Counseling in Redondo Beach, California; Faith Mantooth of Doggie Central in Culver City, California; Cath Phillips from Canine Companions for Independence in Oceanside, California; Catherine Lane of The Possible Canine in Rupert, Quebec; Lani Bray and Rob Condit of Four Paws Play Ranch in Encinitas, California; and Debby Axler of Grateful Dogs Clubhouse in El Segundo, California.

A very special thanks to my fabulous and dear friend Gail Mackenzie-Smith for her countless (and unpaid) hours and good cheer in helping me get this project off the ground, and to Seraphin Canchola, Marni Burns, D.J. MacHale, Richard Curtis, and Grant Biniasz at Veterinary Pet Insurance, for their advice and assistance.

To all the people who contributed their personal stories for this book, I thank you for sharing what, in some cases, were difficult memories to help others keep their beloved dogs safe.

To my mom, Jayne, my dad, Glenn, my sister Ellisa, my brother-in-law Steven, my butt-kicking grannies Honey and Dorris, and my cutie-pies Matthew and Emily. At a time when there were far more important things happening in our family, they remained enthusiastic and interested in the book's progress. I'm grateful to have such amazing love and support.

To TJ, Baylee, Tica, Oreo, Ginger, Millie, Peggy Sue, Hollywood, Timber, Henri, Rocket, Anna, Patch, Genni, and all the dogs that make me smile.

And finally, a big thank you to my sweet, beautiful, happy girl Taiga, who reminds me every day that all you really need in life is food, love, a cushy bed, and a giant tennis ball.

ABOUT THE AUTHOR

Melanie Monteiro is an award-winning advertising writer and voiceover artist in her native Los Angeles. During her twenty-year career, she's worked on many national brands including PetSmart and Pedigree, providing her with a unique insight into the concerns of pet owners, along with an inside glimpse of the pet industry. A lifelong dog lover, Melanie has been a puppy raiser for Canine Companions for Independence, the national organization that provides assistance dogs to people with disabilities. She's also worked as a grooming crew member for the SPCA-LA and is active with other rescue organizations. In her continued quest to help dogs lead safe, healthy lives, Melanie went on to earn certificates in canine nutrition and pet first aid. She currently teaches pet first aid and disaster response courses for the Emergency Care and Safety Institute to pet owners throughout Southern California. Melanie lives in Topanga, California, with her husband, Mark, and Taiga, their six-year-old Lab.

NOTES